THE

The six essays comprising this volume explore the nature and potentials of the art of human living—and how each one of us can pursue it creatively, joyfully, and wisely. They were originally published as separate pamphlets during 1978 and distributed by subscription. This is the first paperback edition.

The significance of these six essays is best attested to by those who have already read them:

"Every essay in *The Art of Living* has been both practical *and* inspirational—a delight to the eye, a comfort to the heart, and a challenge to the mind."
— Jeanne Clark, Ohio

"I believe these essays will continue to be influential for a long time to come. They are a very effective presentation of a new approach to the most fundamental ideas of life."
— Marvin Talsky, D.C., Illinois

"I want to congratulate all of you who have made the essays of *The Art of Living* possible. They are tremendous! Those of us who have the good fortune to have these essays available should be most grateful."
— Roxana Giragossiantz, California

"*The Art of Living* has helped me tremendously in the art of business. If these essays were on every manager's bookshelf, and in every manager's mind, we would have far fewer concerns about productivity, employee relations, and the future of American industry."
— J.R. Gilson, Ohio

The complete series of 30 essays written by Dr. Robert R. Leichtman and Carl Japikse in The Art of Living:

Enriching the Personality
The Practice of Detachment
Finding Meaning in Life
Building Right Human Relationships
The Spirit of Generosity
Joy
Living Responsibly
The Nature and Purpose of the Emotions
Cultivating Tolerance and Forgiveness
Seeking Intelligent Guidance
The Bridge of Faith
Discerning Reality
Cooperating with Life
The Mind and Its Uses: Part I
The Mind and Its Uses: Part II
Coping with Stress
Enlightened Self-Discipline
Inspired Humility: Reverence in Action
The Act of Human Creation: Part I
The Act of Human Creation: Part II
The Work of Patience
The Pursuit of Integrity
The Way to Health: Part I
The Way to Health: Part II
The Process of Self-Renewal
Filling Life with Beauty
Becoming Graceful
The Importance of Courage
The Noblest Masterpiece: Part I
The Noblest Masterpiece: Part II

For information on ordering essays not included in this volume, please turn to page 250.

The Art of Living

VOLUME THREE

A COLLECTION OF ESSAYS
BY ROBERT R. LEICHTMAN, M.D.
& CARL JAPIKSE

With a Foreword
by Nicola M. Tauraso, M.D.

Illustrations by D. Kendrick Johnson

UNITY SCHOOL LIBRARY
UNITY VILLAGE, MISSOURI 64065

ARIEL PRESS
The Publishing House of Light
Columbus, Ohio

No royalties are paid on this book

Copyright © Ariel Press
1978 and 1982
All Rights Reserved

ISBN 0-89804-034-5

*Library of Congress
Card Catalog Number: 81-69186*

Printed in the United States of America

ARIEL PRESS
2557 Wickliffe Road, Columbus, Ohio 43221

TABLE OF CONTENTS

Foreword by Nicola M. Tauraso, M.D. vii

COOPERATING WITH LIFE 1
- The Right Way 3
- Poisonous Attitudes 13
- The Willingness To Share 25
- Changing Our Attitudes 30
- A Partner with God 38

THE MIND AND ITS USES:
Its Nature and Purpose 43
- A Hero's Story 45
- The Full Whir of Activity 49
- Servant of the Soul 72
- The Greatest Discovery 79

THE MIND AND ITS USES:
Its Development and Application 83
- The Lens of the Soul 85
- Missteps on Our Way 90
- Manufacturing Wisdom 106
- The Full Light of Day 117

COPING WITH STRESS ... 123

- A Master of Circumstance ... 125
- The Ingredients of Change ... 136
- The Center of Action ... 148
- Assets in Living ... 153
- The Call of Peace ... 165

ENLIGHTENED SELF-DISCIPLINE ... 169

- A Method of Learning ... 171
- The Wise Parent ... 182
- The Danger of "Letting Go" ... 189
- A Habit of Action ... 198
- Liberating the Spirit ... 206

INSPIRED HUMILITY
Reverence in Action ... 209

- A Robe Without Any Seams ... 211
- A Divisive Force ... 221
- Our Rightful Place ... 227
- Loving God ... 234
- Knowing God ... 241
- Humbling Ourself ... 243

The illustrations in this book were originally published on the covers of each essay, when they appeared as separate pamphlets. They are the work of artist D. Kendrick Johnson of Carmel, California.

A short interpretation of the symbolism of each illustration is printed on the page following it.

FOREWORD

by Nicola M. Tauraso, M.D.

There are many books and essays on human growth and self-realization, but none reaches the degree of perfection attained in *The Art of Living* collection. This series of essays presents the insights of two of the most gifted and creative thinkers I have ever known. Each possesses the ability to perceive psychically the actual nature of human consciousness, which gives their observations a depth of insight seldom found. As a result, there is great power in these essays to help the reader make sense of his or her life—but only if the suggestions set forth in them are given serious attention, consideration, and application. Indeed, the ongoing theme of these essays emphasizes the importance of our attitudes in reaching sensible goals in life, and our need to focus constantly on the God-self within for ultimate expression of our true nature.

The qualifications of both authors are outstanding. As an internist, Dr. Robert R. Leichtman became a courageous seeker of answers lying beyond the meager confines of conventional medicine. By giving wind to his developing clairvoyant abilities, he found he was able to explore a vast new other world of knowledge and truth. As he applied his gifts over the past decade, he has become recognized as the true genius that he is. Carl Japikse found his way to the inner dimensions of knowledge and truth through the channel of creative writing, not medicine, but like Dr. Leichtman has developed remarkable talents and skills in perceiving and understanding human nature and the world around us. Those who read the essays written by this team will understand their message that "human life is rich in creative potential, a potential that can be tapped by *any* man or woman."

Originally, *The Art of Living* essays were published as individual pamphlets, from 1975 through 1980, and distributed as part of an ongoing subscription series. Recently, the first six essays were combined in a paperback edition, Volume I of *The Art of Living*. That was followed by Volume II, comprising essays seven through twelve. Now, essays thirteen through eighteen are being issued in this collection, Volume III.

The first essay in this volume deals with the important concept of "Cooperating with Life." The authors suggest that in order for humans to fulfill their destiny, they must "become active and conscious collaborators with God in the unfoldment of the universe." Since the whole universe functions in a most orderly way, we can achieve this goal only by developing, building, and expressing a cooperative attitude toward all that we do. We must establish a partnership with God, by acting in harmony with the infinite stream of living which is the universe.

The second and third essays deal with "The Mind and Its Uses." Among all the creatures on this planet, we alone have the mind and the capacity to think which enables us to become co-creators with God on earth. This is our unique gift, and it deserves to be honored as such and developed. The authors discuss not only the role of the human mind in advancing civilization, but also state that the mind plays an important part "in the unfoldment of divine consciousness within each one of us individually." The mind is in direct contact with our immortal essence, the soul. Having set forth that basic principle, Dr. Leichtman and Mr. Japikse then explore ways to avoid the pitfalls of fuzzy thinking and truly develop and apply our minds for creative thinking.

In the fourth essay, "Coping with Stress," the authors describe how we can achieve "peace in the midst of suffering." An important purpose of conflict is to stimulate us to apply our creative abilities to establish peace and harmony in our lives. Just as a muscle grows stronger with increasing exercise, we develop an inner psychological strength as we learn to cope wisely with stress. Indeed, many people have experienced great growth during periods of storm and crisis in their lives. God has given us the capacity to grow and develop, and whether stress becomes a negative or a positive force in our lives is determined by our attitudes toward it. The authors are firm in their position that to know peace, we must think peace. The prerequisite is that we become God-centered individuals.

The fifth essay explores the nature and applications of "Enlightened Self-Discipline." With appropriate self-discipline, we become truly responsive to a greater source of wisdom and guidance, thereby increasing our capacity to contribute creatively to civilization. Self-discipline helps the personality reach its highest effectiveness and function.

In the sixth and final essay in this volume, Dr. Leichtman and Mr. Japikse describe how the practice of "Inspired Humility" can fill us with reverence for life, enabling us to carry out our destiny to become co-creators with God. True reverence for life and the whole of creation are qualities of an enlightened human being, and important ingredients in genuine spiritual growth.

It is refreshing to read and digest the ideas put forth in *The Art of Living* series. In our present day, when permissiveness and the lack of self-discipline abound, it is encouraging to know that authors such as Dr. Leichtman and Mr. Japikse are not afraid to share their insights and to state that this or that is what we must do or should not do, in order to achieve our ultimate destiny. Too often, the prevailing advice is that we are free to do whatever we desire—and whenever we wish to do it. These essays, however, go beyond the wish-life, and suggest that there is great order in the universe. To become a part of this orderly unfolding of creation, and to achieve our ultimate human destiny as co-creators with God, we must establish order in our lives and assume responsibility over ourselves and how we live.

I believe there are four important prerequisites to growth: self-responsibility, self-awareness, self-control, and self-discipline. *The Art of Living* is an eloquent statement of how we can activate these four elements of growth, for our own benefit and upward evolution. I readily admit that I enjoy the stimulation I receive from reading and rereading the essays in this volume. It encourages me to act more creatively in practicing the art of *my* living.

Nicola M. Tauraso, M.D. is founder and president of the GOTACH Center for Health in Frederick, Maryland, an educational, research, and treatment facility devoted to healing for the whole person, and author of How To Benefit From Stress *and* Awaken the Genius in Your Child Through Positive Attitude Training.

TO
ARIEL

The Art of Living

COOPERATING WITH LIFE

The great frescoes of the Renaissance were not the work of a single artist, but teams of skillful artists working together, bonded by their love of beauty. Just so, the art of living is not a solitary labor; to be successful in it, we must learn to cooperate — with the soul, with other people, and with the circumstances of life. We must become active and conscious collaborators with God in the unfoldment of the universe.

THE RIGHT WAY

The experiences of the wise and the foolish alike instruct us in a fundamental principle of human living: that reaching our goals is not nearly as important as *reaching them in the right way*. How many people surrender respect, friendship, and their own self-esteem in order to gain wealth and fame, without understanding the personal cost to them? How many examples of spiritual maturity have gained the highest triumphs of all by holding fast to their intangible values, even while scorned and tempted? Achievement alone can be very empty and unsatisfying; to be fulfilling, it must be attained through the noble expression of our humanity. Given this "noble expression," a seeming defeat can often be transformed into a spiritual triumph — for example, by heroically facing overwhelming opposition with courage, goodwill, and dignity. When nobility is abandoned in favor of unethical behavior, however, the apparent victories gained are usually tarnished — and frequently negated. Only the thoughtless applaud the accomplishments of an individual who has won wealth and power through dishonesty, callous disregard of others, and the competitive edge which would kill rather than cooperate. By comparison, the altruistic and unselfish acts of an Albert Schweitzer, a St. Francis, a Luther Burbank, or a Buddha evoke the admiration and reflection of thinking individuals throughout the human race. They inspire us to the right way.

The convictions and attitudes we nurture and express as we move through daily life are the true measure of what we have attained—not material wealth or status. If we are the owner of a garden of despair, hostility, aggressiveness, and selfishness, we have gained nothing to be proud of, no matter how much money or notoriety we possess. If we tend our duties with compassion, tolerance, cheerfulness, and a readiness to share, however, our harvest will be great, whether we appear to succeed or fail.

Approaching life in the right way is one of the principal hallmarks of the art of living, which presupposes that it is *not* enough merely to stumble through each day unintelligently. On the contrary: life is an art form which summons the utmost of our skill, wisdom, and care. Being an art form, life has purpose, meaning, and an intelligent structure. If we choose to ignore these purposes and meanings, we will misunderstand life, and become confused. But if we endeavor to understand and honor them, by cooperating with the laws and principles of living, we will attain success.

Cooperating. It is an easy word to glide over and forget, overlooking its importance. And yet cooperation is the heart of the endeavor to approach life in the right way. We are designed to cooperate. Ultimately, when we have reached a suitable level of genius and spiritual wisdom, we are meant to collaborate with God, consciously and actively. But even before we attain this lofty goal, we are designed to cooperate—with others, with ourself, with the principles of life, and with the right way. It is by cooperating—cooperating with our spouse in creating a loving family environment, cooperating with our spiritual ideals in our daily conduct, and cooperating with the opportunities which come to us—that we grow and become wiser. It is by cooperating—cooperating with our colleagues at work, cooperating with the duties of citizenship and civilization, and cooperating with our own creative destiny—that we become productive and make worthwhile contributions. It is by cooperating—cooperating with the voice of our conscience, cooperating with our own inner drives to set goals and achieve them, and cooperating with the right way—that we make a success of our efforts. Even in the smallest of ways, it is important to learn to cooperate. For just as a pianist can only hope to play compositions demanding great skill if he has first practiced on many simple etudes, we can only hope to learn the secrets of cooperating with God if we first master the skills of cooperating with others, cooperating with our best motives and attitudes, and cooperating with our opportunities.

Sadly, many people do not clearly see the value of cooperation. They devote themselves to the selfish manipulation of a world they feel to be hostile and ready to defeat them—if they do not defeat it first. Such people go through life believing themselves to be the victims of some ongoing war with others and with society. They expend enormous amounts of time and energy in erecting fail-safe defense mechanisms or in being unnecessarily competitive; they become obsessed with the importance of *winning* and develop a sadistic lust to see others lose. Not uncommonly, these people believe that the only way to succeed is to intimidate and oppose others and coldly throttle any instinct within themselves to be generous and considerate.

It is true that there are hostile, paranoid, and criminal people in the world, but it does not require hostility, paranoia, or criminality of our own to avoid being victimized by them. Indeed, such attitudes are distinctly the "wrong ways" of reaching success; they greatly imperil the quality of life. People who espouse the notion of winning by intimidation and opposition succeed only in eliminating the very character traits which provide a sense of fulfillment, significance, and worth. They estrange themselves from the helpfulness and kindness which is innate in most of their fellow human beings. Along the way, they become friendless and abandoned—surrounded only by other selfish predators who stand ready to snatch away their ill-gotten "treasures" at the slightest show of weakness. Ironically, these people completely fail to perceive that success can almost always be achieved far more easily through the routes of cooperation and honesty than through the elaborate shams and devious means which must be constantly devised to keep all the other wolves from their door.

Some of the best examples of this utter selfishness can be found in the activities of the so-called "robber barons" who dealt in stock market speculation a hundred years ago—people such as Jay Gould. Gould was guided by one motive alone—his personal profit. He mercilessly destroyed the careers of others, corrupted public officials to gain special favors, and drained healthy businesses of their funds, leaving them bankrupt and useless. He caused massive financial panics and widespread suffering. To quote one description, he "remained ruthless, unscrupulous, and friendless to the end."

And yet, other individuals have built fortunes even greater than Gould's employing far more humanistic and creative means. They have brought talented people into their organizations and given them responsible positions. They have worked to establish useful businesses which serve the needs of society and their customers, rather than leeching existing businesses that they have purchased cheaply through deceit. They have supported and encouraged responsible involvement in society and government, instead of seeking advancement through corruption and undermining democracy. They have sounded the keynote of cooperation and have proven that it works.

Not all people who have yet to see the full value of cooperation are quite the vultures of intimidation and opposition Jay Gould was, of course. Selfishness, intimidation, and hostility come in many shades and intensities. Some people specialize in expressing their uncooperativeness at home, where they set themselves up as petty tyrants who bully and manipulate everyone else. Others attack the unity of groups to which they belong, by being antagonistic and critical of every idea proposed. And there are many individuals who are able to cooperate effectively with others, but cannot cooperate with themselves; they sabotage their own best efforts through incessant doubt, cowardice, and confusion.

These are just variations on a common theme, however. The lack of cooperation produces the same result in all circumstances—the impoverishment of consciousness. The signs of noncooperation never vary. Uncooperative people can be spotted *by what they lack*.

They lack a sense of ethics; they have few inner moral convictions to guide their behavior. This deficiency goes much deeper than just lacking good manners—it is a failure to see that there is a right way of treating other people and a definite responsibility on the part of each of us to life—a responsibility to do things wisely and compassionately. Because of this lack of ethics, selfish people always define the "best option" in terms of personal expediency, ignoring the interests of others and of society. What they fail to realize is that personal expediency is not a principle recognized by the universe; decisions made on this basis will invariably backfire, at least in the long term.

Uncooperative people also lack compassion and the ability to care about the well-being of others. This self-centered attitude can be seen, for example, in parents who ridicule and embarrass their children as though they were their personal toys, or managers who regard their staff as personal minions.

They lack an understanding of how cooperating with other people and with their own humanity can benefit them. They are so obsessed with the importance of their self-advancement that they have not bothered to take the time to observe the models of advancement in the universe—which are all based on the principle of cooperation.

They lack faith in themselves, in their human and spiritual potential, in God, and in the order of the universe. Consequently, they do not even have the *means* for cooperation. How is it possible to cooperate with someone else if we do not have at least a token of faith in his abilities, good intentions, or friendship? How is it possible to cooperate with life if we do not have faith that life has purpose and significance?

They lack the courage to do and say the things they know are fair and mutually beneficial. Cowardice is a great block to cooperation, for it is the paralyzing inability to cooperate with our own highest self.

And they lack the commitment of responsibility. Responsibility is the ability to make a meaningful response to our obligations and duties—to spouse, family, employer, community, nation, and humanity as a whole. Uncooperative people do not respond; they intimidate, they oppose, they withdraw, and they divide.

Of course, to state that uncooperative people can be categorized by what they do not have is only half the story; it is equally true that cooperative people are characterized by the riches they possess—riches of human consciousness, friendship, and ever-increasing opportunity. The principle at work is the classic division between the "haves" and the "have nots"; those who have mastered the cooperative spirit of living are blessed with great abundance, while those who have not are cursed by their own impoverished attitudes.

Cooperative people are enriched by a strong sense of ethics. They know the kind of behavior the universe rewards, and act accordingly. As a result, they are constantly receiving the dividends of their enlightened behavior, and their richness grows, while others wonder why.

Cooperative people are also enriched by a deep concern for the well-being of others. They seek to help and assist, whenever possible. As a result, others become genuinely interested in helping and assisting them, whenever support is needed.

Cooperative people delight in the accomplishments of others, and help promote them, knowing that through these contributions the whole of humanity will be enriched, and therefore their own lives. They also know that by helping the good ideas and plans of others take root and grow, they are establishing genuine bonds of friendship.

Cooperative people are enriched by a steady measure of faith — in their own potential, the capacities of others, and the destiny of the universe. As a result, they do not become discouraged when they or others falter. They have the resources of enlightened faith to help them overcome setbacks.

Cooperative people possess the treasure of courage, too. Being in the habit of cooperating with their higher self, they are aware of its great strength supporting their self-expression.

And cooperative people are enriched with a strong sense of responsibility. As a result, they are continually being asked to accept new responsibilities, for they have demonstrated the ability to be a proper guardian of success. They attract to themselves meaningful opportunities and the support they need to capitalize on them.

Enriched in these ways, cooperative people are able to grow in skill, understanding, and maturity. They become increasingly aware of and attuned to the great human purpose which is ripening and unfolding in everything they do. Even a glimmer of this purpose is worth all of the glamour of power and wealth which can be amassed.

The selfish and ignorant are likely to scoff at a statement of this nature. And yet, when all the material wealth and fleeting power of the selfish and ignorant have passed away, the compassion, caring, faith, and courage of people who cooperate with life will endure. Such qualities of the art of living last forever. They do not fade or die; instead, they grow and multiply.

Cooperation is a tool which helps us learn more about our humanity and how to express it. The lessons of human competence are not learned in isolated towers; they are mastered by interacting with our fellow human beings. We cannot possibly hope to learn who we are unless we simultaneously learn to deal responsibly and maturely with our "companions along the way," any more than a sculptor can hope to create a great work of art without a block of stone or wood to carve. Our attitudes toward others, ourself, and the events of our life *are* the raw materials, the blocks of granite, that we use in the art of living.

Nor can a sculptor hope to create his masterpieces of beauty by antagonistically fighting the basic nature of his raw material, working, for example, against the grain of a piece of wood. He must cooperate with the wood the way it is. Just so, we must discover that cooperation is the basic attitude which lets us profit from our relationships with others, our communion with ourself, and our opportunities for achievement.

Because cooperation is founded upon purposeful living, the expression of it naturally adds purpose to everything we do. A marriage which is founded on competition and conflict will have little purpose and even less satisfaction. But a marriage based on cooperation, upon building a mutual expression of love, will radiate a profound sense of purpose. It will be fulfilling and joyful, not because it was "made in heaven" but because the two participants have worked maturely together to create something worthwhile.

Simply put, cooperation is the way the universe works. We have the freedom to isolate ourself from humanity, from our opportunities, and from our own greatness; we can choose the paths of intimidation, deceit, and opposition if we so desire. But these are merely limitations and restrictions we impose upon ourself. Under no conditions can we impose them upon the universe in which we live. And so, even though we may erect barriers of selfishness, the universe continues as before. We may think we will not cooperate with life, *but life cooperates with us!* If we practice selfishness, it cooperates with us by giving us the consequences of selfishness. If we antagonize our friends, it cooperates with us by seeing to it that we are friendless. If we cheat, it cooperates with us most poetically by arranging circumstances in which we will be cheated. If we tyrannize our spouse, it cooperates with us by making sure that we will be equally matched in our tyrannical battles sometime in the future. Of course, these opportunities will be of such a frighteningly low grade that they will be distinctly unappealing. We probably would not even call them opportunities.

We have been designed to collaborate with life, and life is intent on collaborating with us. As might be expected, if we adapt our attitudes so that we live life in the right way—if we nurture the attitude of cooperation—then we will find this collaboration with life a great blessing. If we are helpful with our co-workers, the universe will cooperate with us by helping us in times of need. If we work with our spouse to create a home environment in which our children can evolve into competent, compassionate adults, the universe will cooperate with us by opening new horizons for our growth. If we sense our responsibility in community and nation and work to further the goals and purposes of society, the universe will cooperate with us by providing opportunities for greater influence. If we honor and respect our own destiny and potential for greatness, the universe will cooperate with us in ways that most people cannot even imagine.

Nor is it necessary for us to imagine what it means to be a partner with God. Reality has a marvelous way of transcending the mere imaginations of the inexperienced. What is important is understanding that cooperation *makes sense* as an attitude to life. Similarly, the attitudes of intimidation, defensiveness, and separativeness do not make sense, because they are the antithesis of cooperation. They are wasteful and stupid, the products of ignorance, laziness, and selfishness. To attain genuine and fulfilling achievements, we must learn the lessons of cooperating with life.

POISONOUS ATTITUDES

As Paul wrote in I Corinthians 2:9, "Eye has not seen nor ear has not heard the glories that God has prepared for those who love Him." The universe is benevolent both by nature and in function; it is filled with an abundance of good things. Being creatures of the universe, we are destined to share in this abundance. When we fail to do so, it is primarily due to the limitations and restrictions we place on ourselves, by opposing life. This opposition can take many forms — intimidation, hostility, and deceit — but its underlying theme is the lack of cooperation. It is therefore important to consider why people become uncooperative. Is it not odd that so many people deny themselves the rich blessings, both tangible and intangible, of their birthright? Why do people choose hardship and impoverishment of consciousness, when they could chose the treasures of heaven?

One reason is **ignorance.** Uncooperative people do not understand that life is benevolent, that they are linked with this benevolence through the strands of their own divinity, and that cooperation is one of the basic patterns through which everything is built in this universe. Nor do they realize that they have the capacity to heal others, to console others, or to enrich the lives of others in any way. Of course, they are ignorant only because they have not troubled themselves to think. If a person takes time to think, it is hard *not* to see that the universe is benevolent, cooperation is rewarded, and we are designed to share life with others. The signs and signals are everywhere; they surround us and beg us constantly to pay heed.

A second reason is **laziness.** Even though the universe is filled with blessings of all kinds, it does require active involvement on our part to tap these blessings. Some people, however, are unwilling to invest any effort in life, even if the reward compensates their time and trouble one hundredfold. They prefer to live the life of a parasite, comfortably believing that they are getting something for nothing. More accurately, they are getting nothing for nothing. Giving nothing to the universe, the universe cooperates perfectly with them by giving them nothing in return.

By its very nature, cooperation implies the willingness to share our efforts with others. Curiously, as we do, our ability to receive the blessings of the universe increases much more rapidly than if we expended the same effort individually. But all of this is lost on the lazy person, who cultivates an uncooperative attitude simply because he cannot be bothered to contribute to life.

The major reason why people become uncooperative is **selfishness.** Many people dimly sense that cooperation involves a certain spirit of sacrifice, without having any notion of just what sacrifice entails. They are afraid of cooperating with others, because they imagine they will have to give up something. Sadly, most people who are selfish in this way have very little worth holding onto — especially when compared with the riches of life in the universe, riches which could be theirs if they were not so selfish. Sometimes, these selfish people hold onto material possessions they might share with others, but most frequently they cling to overrated psychological possessions—vanity, a sense of independence, self-importance, fears, and the desire to have things their way all the time. As they cling, they become paranoid, coldly eyeing every other human being as an enemy interested only in taking away from them that which they cherish. In such a climate, sharing and cooperation become impossible.

Some people believe that by being deliberately uncooperative—and even intimidating—they have found the key to success and fulfillment. But because the attitude of noncooperation is grounded in ignorance, laziness, and selfishness, such a notion is obviously without substance. Indeed, a lack of cooperation is the *barrier* to genuine success and fulfillment. Only by cooperating with the benevolent and harmonious elements in ourself and in life can we gain access to the storehouse of abundance and prosperity that is the universe. If life, or any part of it, is treated as an enemy to be overwhelmed or tricked, then we are estranging ourself from the very source of fulfillment. We are spurning a fundamental principle of the universe, and are foolishly setting ourself up for disappointment and misery. Even if we should conquer and control some small aspect of life, so that it is virtually enslaved to us, we still would not have attained the power or posture which would let us enjoy this "triumph." The gains obtained through intimidation, dishonesty, or domination are unstable gains, for they are always in danger of being lost or stolen by someone else, should we lose control of our little empire—even for a minute. Thus, fear undermines the pleasure of success; the need to defend and protect our ill-gotten gains diminishes the happiness we thought would come with them. *Satisfaction in life and the full realization of our human potential can never be stolen or obtained illicitly. They can be achieved only by cooperating with life.*

These three basic ingredients of noncooperation—ignorance, laziness, and selfishness—tend to combine alchemically with one another, producing in turn a number of sulphurous potions which poison the way we interact with life. In every instance, they drug consciousness and inhibit mature growth. These poisons, along with their effects and antidotes, are:

Defensiveness. Some people believe that we live in a hostile world and must be ready to neutralize the manipulativeness of others. So they withdraw into a protective shell, unwilling to help others lest they be taken advantage of, unwilling to cultivate friendships for fear of becoming vulnerable. This is defensiveness, a self-perpetuating attitude; for as we regard others as unfriendly and unhelpful, we automatically push them away. We prevent them from coming to our aid when we need assistance. Even if they are good-hearted and seek us out, we are unlikely to believe they are sincere. Schooled in defensiveness, we assume that they are seeking to crack our protective wall. We pull our shell of defensiveness more tightly about us.

The regrettable consequence of defensiveness is *loneliness*—and in extreme cases, when defensiveness has become paranoia, *aloneness*. Believing that we live in a hostile world, we make little effort to befriend it or any of its inhabitants. As a result, we generate a state of not having any genuine friends—friends with whom we can share our life, our hopes, our dreams, and our successes; friends we can rely on to help at critical times. This kind of loneliness is a psychological state, not a physical condition. Lonely people are often surrounded by many other human beings—their family, acquaintances and colleagues at work. But through their defensiveness, they gradually alienate all of the many people in their life. They may still have some avenues of communication open to a few of these people, but usually these ties are only to others of a like attitude—other defensive and hostile people. And so, their loneliness is aggravated.

Far worse is the state of aloneness. At this point, we have come to believe that there is no one in the world, no thing in the world, and no thing within ourself which can help us. Aloneness is a state of bitter despair wherein we separate ourself from *everything* of value. It is a devastating condition of ignorance, founded on strident paranoia. We disown even God and the intelligence of the universe, believing that He cannot and will not help us. As a result, we end up totally alone and isolated—severed from beauty, purpose, and fulfillment. Aloneness is a desolate state, one which has rightly been labeled the most serious of cardinal sins.

Loneliness and aloneness are self-inflicted wounds. The friendless, uncooperative person will probably insist that his loneliness is the fault of everyone else, thereby increasing his hostility and defensiveness—but the truth of the matter is otherwise.

The cure for this unpleasant state of being is to cultivate friendliness and a cooperative attitude. We must shed our ignorance and selfishness and realize that it *is* worthwhile to be friendly. Then, we must start accepting others as they are, for better or for worse. We must abandon our defensiveness and see others as possible friends who have just as much potential interest in us as we have in them; we can benefit from being friendly with them as much as they can benefit from being friendly with us. Having nothing left to lose but our loneliness, we must see that there is much of substance to be gained by sharing life with others. In this way, we undercut the former strength of our selfishness, clearing the atmosphere for decent and friendly overtures which can lead to valuable friendships.

Self-deprivation. This poison is a strong concoction, a masochistic blending of ignorance and laziness, based on the wholly erroneous assumption that there are not enough opportunities, blessings, and goodwill to meet the needs of everyone. We conclude, therefore, that it is our lot in life to do without and be deprived. Guided by such attitudes of defeat, we choose not to cooperate with the opportunities which come to us, or the universe, or our own talents and skills.

Self-deprivation is amazingly prevalent. On the physical level, it is the basis of the so-called "welfare attitude" and the widespread lack of genuine generosity. Emotionally, many people practice self-deprivation by not aspiring to the joy, peace, and fulfillment which are the heritage of all human beings. As long as they do not have serious problems, they are content; some people even manage to be content with misery and suffering, mostly because they cannot be troubled to make the effort to strive for something better. Mentally, self-deprivation is typified by the attitude of the person who finds a safe, comfortable job in which he or she can stagnate for the rest of life, steering clear of any new challenges or the need to develop additional skills. Spiritually, it can be seen in the alarming attitude that we are worthless, sinful, miserable creatures who must grovel at the feet of a spiteful God who will occasionally toss us a few scraps of "grace" if we will repeat His name often enough. Another manifestation of spiritual self-deprivation is the notion that since we are so wicked, we must "get ourself out of the way," usually by practicing what is known as "self-denial."

The central problem with self-deprivation is that it leads people to act as though they will not achieve anything worthwhile in life except by a lucky accident or a miraculous act of God. They train themselves to have unbelievably low expectations, and therefore become inactive and disinterested in doing anything either to help themselves or to make a valuable contribution to the life of humanity.

The effect of self-deprivation is to impoverish opportunities, ideals, and consciousness. If indulged in, it eventually leads to states of despair and depression, for life seems barren and unfulfilling. This illusion of barrenness in turn creates a further sense of emptiness in thought, feeling, and aspiration, and the cycle deepens. Truly, people who victimize themselves in this way are "poor in spirit." They fail to see the infinite blessings of life.

The antidote for self-deprivation is to cooperate with our own faith, talent, and blessings. It takes skill and effort to receive the blessings of life. We are privileged to sup at the banquet table of God, but God does not wait on us as though He were a member of the household staff! We must serve ourself if we are to receive His bounty. We must come to realize that the opportunities and riches of the universe are infinite, and each of us has an infinite share in them. There is no limit to the talent, the love and compassion, the dignity, or the sense of brotherhood we can develop — not even a limit to the opportunities we can invoke. The only limits in life are the ones we place on ourself, through our laziness and incorrect attitudes—through our self-deprivation.

Exploitation. Whereas self-deprivation is the attitude that "there is not enough to go around, so we must do without," exploitation is the more lethal poison that "there is not enough to go around, so we must steal what we can from someone else." Not content with enduring their limited circumstances (which they have unknowingly created themselves), the exploiters of the world choose to take what they want from others. Such people shun ethical ways of dealing with life in favor of scheming, manipulation, and dishonesty—and rationalize that this behavior is necessary because "everyone else is doing it." Instead of cooperating with others for everyone's mutual benefit, they become fiercely competitive, putting a premium on winning and forcing others to lose.

The most obvious example of exploitation is criminal behavior. But there are other, more subtle forms of exploitation which, although not proscribed by law, are nonetheless contrary to the spirit of cooperation. It is exploitation, for example, when an individual tries to steal the romantic affection of someone already attached to another person. Similarly, it is exploitation when someone deliberately tries to take away another person's job or drive a competitor out of business. While it is perfectly ethical and desirable to aspire to pleasant companionship, a fulfilling job, and a productive business, it is not right to attain any of these goals by stealing them.

Fierce competitiveness is often used by the exploiter to obtain his or her ends. This does not mean, however, that all competition is bad. Actually, friendly competition is a valuable and healthy aspect of cooperation, as it can help us aspire to the development of our highest potential and talent. By competing *with* people for academic, athletic, or spiritual prizes, we help everyone involved sharpen his skills and achieve greater competence. Without competition, we would not be able to progress as rapidly along our path of destiny; it often helps to link us with our higher self and transform the personality. But competing *against* other people is destructive and unethical. Such competition is not the right way of doing things, no matter how prized the objective. It tears down the principle of cooperation and opens the door for exploitation. It encourages people to covet what others have and secretly scheme to obtain it. It makes defeating the other person the object of the competition — not creating a stronger link with our soul and with life.

The consequences of exploitation are grim but just — the universe gives us exactly what we have given it. If we steal from others, we can expect to forfeit something of equal value. If we grab the opportunities of others, our opportunities will turn sour. If we cheat, we will be taken advantage of in return. In criminal cases, the officers of the law are the channels for this correction. But compensation occurs even in the most subtle cases, although it may not be immediately apparent. Exploitative people dig a big hole of debts to the universe and then fall into it, trapped.

In addition, such people are constantly vulnerable to the wrath, retaliation, and vengeance of the people they have exploited. Consequently, what they do achieve in this unethical way cannot be fully enjoyed, for there is a constant fear that their lack of ethics will be exposed — and they will lose all which they have gained.

It is not easy for exploitative people to change their habits, but it can be done. Again, the key is changing their attitudes and realizing that cooperation is the right way to do things—and will, in the long run, produce the greatest gains and the most satisfaction. A respect for ethical behavior must be cultivated.

Domination and **possession.** While slavery and servitude are no longer legal, there are nonetheless many people who wish they still were. These are individuals who are not content with stealing what others have through clever scheming and trickery; they lust for outright domination. They want to possess totally what the other person has and reduce that person to the role of marionette. Domination runs the gamut from treachery and blackmail on the one extreme to the demand for total possession of a "loved" one on the other—the common notion that marriage gives us ownership of the other person's body, affection, feelings, and mind. In all cases, domination is achieved by oppressing and denying the free will of the other person. Wherever it is found, it is the sign of an intensely sick relationship—the direct opposite of cooperation.

Domination and possession are maintained through the use of intimidation, threats of great loss or harm, and psychological blackmail. The threat is often couched in friendly terms, but if it is ignored, the friendliness disappears and the true vicious nature of the person seeking domination comes to the surface. One of the most subtle expressions of domination is in the realm of the mind, with one person trying to control and brainwash the thoughts and beliefs of another, or of a group of people. Many fringe religious cults practice this form of domination, as do individuals without a sense of ethics.

The consequences of domination and possession are much the same as those of exploitation, only more pronounced. This attitude toward life produces a smugness which poisons the perception of life, until the dominating person becomes addicted to his or her passion. It creates a state of psychological vampirism which ironically makes the dominating person totally dependent upon his victims, for if he loses them, he loses his sense of control. He also loses his basic sustenance, and collapses in abject agony.

The only antidote for this deplorable state is realizing that each human being is a child of God, blessed with a rich inheritance. Rather than standing in the way of anyone enjoying that inheritance directly, by trying to take it for ourself, we must dedicate ourself to helping others learn about this heritage. We must give up our vampiristic ways and learn that it is much more satisfying to drink from the universal fountain, one among many drinking together.

Irresponsibility. This, too, is one of the poisons of uncooperativeness. It can be found in business when one employee shirks his work, forcing others to compensate for him. It can be encountered in marriages, when one spouse leaves all the duties of the home to the other. It can be seen in the relationship of individuals to society when people do not fulfill their obligations as citizens, when they do not cooperate with the laws of the land, and when they take the attitude that courts are avenues not for justice but for self-aggrandizement. Irresponsibility is typified by the currently popular attitude that we have the right to make up our own rules of living as we go along and to change them at any time it seems expedient to do so.

The effect of irresponsibility is *confusion*. With essentially selfish goals and no ethics to guide him, the irresponsible person views the world as a chaotic and bewildering place. And since he is constantly adapting his "rules" to suit the needs of the moment, he is soon lost in a vast sea of unending contradictions and paradoxes.

The remedy for irresponsibility lies in a greater devotion to learning to do things in the right way and becoming more responsive to the purposes of the soul. We must learn to cooperate with our own inner direction in life and then honor this cooperation by caring about people, our work, and our country.

Each of these five poisons of noncooperation, their effects, and their cures can also be seen to operate within the realm of groups, religions, businesses, and nations. Defensiveness, for instance, has been a problem for thousands of years in the Hebrew race, causing it to suffer an unequaled loneliness and state of separation among the races and nations of the world. Indeed, this defensiveness long ago became sufficiently paranoid to create a sad history of persecution. Self-deprivation can be seen in the uncooperative attitude of the major religions toward one another, each claiming to be "the way" and rejecting the validity of the other approaches. As a result, each ends up clinging to a tiny fragment of the blessings of the world, unable to share and rejoice in the mutual blessings which have been bestowed on all peoples, all parts of the earth. Exploitation is so common that it is difficult to cite only one or two examples. Certainly the caste system of the Hindus is one classic case, as are all wars waged throughout history for the purpose of grabbing territory from other nations and peoples. In the realm of domination and possession, we need to look no further than the repressive totalitarian regimes of communism, which seek to annihilate any vestige of free will in their people while establishing special privileges for an elite that is supported by a system of virtual slavery. This is "justified" on the grounds that they are creating a socialist society which totally supplies the needs of the population, but the needs supplied in this fashion are only animal needs for physical survival. Spiritual needs are ignored; in fact, they are deliberately sabotaged by the establishment of militantly atheistic societies. Finally, poignant examples of irresponsibility can be seen almost daily in the conduct of many of the members of the United Nations, who change the rules to suit their needs and weaken, through childish petulance, what could be an institution of great importance.

Whether on a global or a personal scale, the unwillingness to cooperate with life is still poisonous. It seeps insidiuously into our thoughts and behavior, attacking the very source of life within us—our connections with the soul. When we refuse to cooperate as we should, we destroy some part of the vital humanity within us. And yet, if we have been uncooperative with life in the past, it is not a cause for despair. The spread of the poison can be stopped. We can renew our ties with the soul and learn to cooperate with life even as the soul does, at its own level. Through dedicated effort, we can build a cooperative spirit in our own thoughts and feelings, and thereby reestablish our rightful claim to share in the benevolence and abundance of the universe.

THE WILLINGNESS TO SHARE

The word "cooperation" defines itself. We co-*operate* by operating or acting mutually with other people and the resources of life, in a specific project, activity, or aspect of living. Such cooperation is more than just joint participation, however; the state of togetherness can lead as easily to conditions of domination and manipulation as to genuine cooperation. Rather, it implies that everyone involved in an activity is contributing something of value to its direction, management, or fulfillment. In return, each is receiving benefit and satisfaction, and has a mutual awareness of responsibility—even though the levels of responsibility may vary from one person to the next. For the spirit of cooperation to flourish and bear fruit, we must care about the scope and effectiveness of the contributions which others make, as well as our own. We must share with others the good elements which enrich our own life—our talents, friendliness, goodwill, joy, compassion, wisdom, and peace. This willingness to share the best within us is really the heart of cooperating with life. It establishes us as a contributor to life, rather than a parasite on the productivity of others, and therefore enables us to share in the abundance and benevolence of *all life*.

Enlightened cooperation, in other words, is *mutual expressiveness*. It is an inherently active state, springing from the aspiration to achieve a more fulfilling involvement in life. It is this characteristic of cooperation which makes it so vital to the art of living—and to all forms of creativity. An individual working by himself is tremendously limited in his capacity to create or accomplish anything. At the very least, he must learn to cooperate with his own talents, inspiration, resources, purpose, and ethics. But the range of his creativity and contributions widens enormously if he also learns to cooperate with the blessings and opportunities of the universe. If, in addition, he cultivates the capacity to cooperate with other people, as well as entities beyond the human kingdom, his possibilities for creative achievement become virtually limitless.

This concept of enlightened cooperation, however, excludes a number of practices often mistaken for "cooperation." Cooperation is not a state of mindless selflessness, for example, where we deny everything of value within ourself and surrender to another person, a business partner, a religious leader, or even God. God does not actually want idiotic sycophants as partners of life; He chooses intelligent, highly-skilled individuals who know who they are and how they can assist in the grand scheme of evolution.

Nor is cooperation a state of groveling permissiveness, where we allow others to do anything which pleases them on the grounds that interfering with them would be "uncooperative." Unfortunately, many people do confuse permissiveness with cooperation. It has become popular, for example, to advise people: "You do your thing, and I will do mine, and if we happen to share the same experience, great." Such statements, however, usually carry with them a rather threatening overtone: "If you do *not* let me do my thing, I'll make damned sure you don't get a chance to do yours."

Some people live so superficially that they mistake cooperation for simple niceness and politeness. If they share nice, warm feelings with their spouse, they believe they are being cooperative. If they hug someone at church, they think they love mankind. Cooperating with life, however, requires more than just feeling good about it. It is not a question of how we feel, but rather what we do and how we do it. The cooperative person is involved in life, supporting noble endeavors, helping people grow, and working in harmony with his inner spirit.

At the other end of the scale, there are some people

who are so self-centered that every concept they encounter soon becomes twisted into a justification for self-indulgence. In the name of cooperating with the higher self, for example—and with a perfect conscience—they will insist that they must have special advantages, privileged treatment, and all manner of dispensation from the rules and regulations the rest of us must honor. Such people have a real talent for forgetting that everyone else has a higher self, too.

Others approach cooperation as a calculated, self-centered investment of time and energy designed to procure the attention, sympathy, and goodwill of others. Far from being motivated by a willingness to share, it is just another instance of the wolf of exploitation dressing himself in pretty lambskins, in order to make his preying easier. Let it suffice to observe that the spirit of cooperation never involves surrendering to intimidation of any kind, no matter how subtle, in spite of what most labor unions, warring nations, criminals, and self-assertive therapists seem to believe. Cooperation is an expression of goodwill, friendliness, and caring. It is rooted in the highest attitudes and ethics of our being, and impels us to make a worthwhile contribution through our duties, friendships, and participation in life.

If the spirit of cooperation is genuine, it will be found at all levels. It will be found at the physical level, as illustrated in the tremendous cooperation required among members of a trapeze troupe or the individuals in a mountain climbing expedition—or in thousands of less exotic situations. But cooperation is just as important emotionally. It is an indispensable ingredient in the give-and-take rapport of marriage, family, and friendships. So many marriages and friendships suffer because the participants only co-exist; they do not cooperate. They do not work together to nurture and develop the emotional and psychic rapport which truly forms a relationship. In much the same way, good morale in a group is largely dependent upon the ability of its members to respect one another and work together efficiently toward the group's goals. Where there is bad morale, the major problem is always a lack of cooperation.

Cooperation also plays a significant role at the level of the mind and ideas. It involves having the courage to support and defend others who voice noble and important ideas, encouraging people with good ideas to develop them, and using our intelligence to counsel, console, and heal people in need of assistance. The mental level of cooperation is likewise a key to the development of an enlightened spirit of community and citizenship.

But nowhere is the willingness to share more clearly expressed than at the spiritual level, where it develops within us a sense of kinship with spirit — not only within ourself but with others as well. Unfortunately, many people who earnestly seek spiritual growth have serious problems learning to cooperate with the force of that growth. They want the benefits of the spiritual life, but on their own terms. And so they refuse to listen to the teaching made available to them, hearing only the echoes of their own long-standing habits of self-centeredness and desire. They do not cooperate with the promptings of their higher intelligence, because they have formed preconceived notions about what must be done, and when, and how.

To cooperate with spirit, be it our own or the spirit manifesting through others, we must rise above the pettiness which has dominated us, to appreciate and respect the *purposes* of life, the *ethics* of living, and the *right way* of acting and behaving. Where our attitudes are lacking, we must adjust them. Where our involvement in life has been fainthearted, we must strengthen it.

We must practice the willingness to share. For when we do, we will understand our kinship with life, and know the role we play in it.

CHANGING OUR ATTITUDES

Cooperation is an attitude toward living—an attitude of desiring to approach life always in the right way. The measure of our cooperation is therefore determined entirely by our own willingness. To increase it, we must be willing to update and improve our own beliefs, attitudes, and convictions, so that they are more in harmony with *the way life is*. Primarily, we need to work to neutralize the three causes of non-cooperation: ignorance, laziness, and selfishness.

Ignorance is defeated as we cultivate an awareness of the benevolence of spirit and the underlying unity of all life. It is never easy to erase ignorance, for it breeds in our prejudices, superstitions, hurt feelings, and pet beliefs. Why cooperate, the voice of ignorance wonders, with someone we do not like, someone who cannot be trusted, or someone we fear? Indeed, why cooperate with the universe—what has it done for us?

Such are the taunts of ignorance. They are overcome by learning about the nature and strength of the soul—the creative, loving, and divine impulse within us. As we discover that the soul is a source of unlimited support, guidance, wisdom, love, joy, and power, we begin to understand why it is useful to cooperate with it. As we realize that the universe in which the soul lives and moves and has its being is an orderly, intelligent, and just system of life, we begin to comprehend what it has done for us—and why it is useful to act ethically. And as we find that everyone else has similar connections to the soul and to the universe, we begin to understand why it is useful to cooperate with others—even people we do not care for. In fact, we realize we *must* cooperate with life and the people we share it with, if we are to fulfill our heritage and receive the blessings of our birthright. So we shed the coat of our ignorance.

Laziness is overcome by strengthening our motivation to cooperate. To succeed, however, we will have to approach this change in attitude with a great deal of enthusiasm, for the weight of inertia and lethargy can be heavy indeed. It is much easier to do nothing at all than to develop a refined set of ethics, or work at improving the quality of our marriage, or cooperate with our inner potential. But doing nothing at all is not a healthy option; it causes stagnation and loss.

The best way to strengthen our motivation to cooperate is by considering the benefits we will receive as we become more cooperative. These benefits are many and varied: greater peace of mind, better treatment from others, a closer rapport with the soul, more satisfying friendships with others, a deeper sense of fulfillment from responsibilities and creative accomplishments, and the opportunities which come from a higher level of ethical living. Contemplating these good returns on our investment should suffice to stir up our enthusiasm to meet life with renewed interest, fairness, and cooperation. It should help us see the value of evolving a code of ethics, a respect for responsibility, and a willingness to help and share. In building this motivation, however, it is important to avoid energizing ulterior motives—by deciding, for example, that cooperating with others will enable us to manipulate them all the more easily. Such a motive would indicate we are still in the grips of laziness, believing it to be easier to achieve success through trickery and conniving than through honest and ethical means.

One of the most effective methods of increasing right motivation is to spend time nurturing a deep and healthy respect for other people—especially the ones we are to cooperate with. If we can respect the contributions they make, the fairness and compassion with which they treat us, the joy they add to our life, the intelligence they manifest, and their other human qualities, we will find it much easier to build a cooperative attitude.

Selfishness is neutralized by learning to appreciate the common goals and purposes we share with others in our mutual endeavors. As long as we focus on our differences and personal needs, cooperation will be impossible. But if we take the time to remember why we are involved in an activity or project—and what we hope to accomplish—we will find it possible to defuse our selfishness. Many marriages, for example, degenerate into contests of who can insult or dominate the other more ingeniously. If the partners in such marriages would quietly reflect on how much they have invested in each other, however, they would soon see the waste and immaturity of such competition. Usually, they have invested a major portion of their lives and a good deal of sacrifice in raising their children, creating a home, and shaping a meaningful relationship. When two lives are so inextricably intertwined, why damage them through selfish conflict? To hurt one is to hurt both. By recognizing these underlying themes of purpose, they will find it easier to transcend their selfishness and begin building anew upon their common purposes and shared goals.

Labor-management struggles are another illustration of two sides trying to destroy one another, when they should be mutually working to achieve the common goals which serve them both. Unions paint the industry employing them as an enemy, and management often feels the same toward the unions. And so they line up with their self-serving interests and hurl abuse at one another, poles apart. This kind of absurd selfishness can only be overcome by realizing that the mutual benefits of cooperating to supply a needed product or service far outweigh any individual interests. Without this realization, the selfish demands of both parties will destroy the industry and everyone concerned.

Another weapon in the arsenal against selfishness is to learn to make meaningful and reasonable sacrifices, as circumstances require them. In fact, sacrifice is an inseparable part of cooperation; it is hard to imagine any kind of meaningful mutual expression without the people involved being willing to give up something they value—time, energy, pet notions, old habits, and so on.

Many people are afraid of the implications of sacrifice, but it is only when selfishness holds sway that sacrifice seems unpleasant or distasteful. The unselfish person rejoices in the sacrifices he makes, because he understands he is willingly foregoing something he values *in order to receive or achieve something much better in exchange!* We sacrifice some of our independence when we marry because we know that the mutual benefits of marriage are well worth the exchange. How silly it is, then, for selfish people to try to cling to their old independence and thereby jeopardize all they have hoped for! In becoming parents, we sacrifice much of our free time and assume a variety of responsibilities. But the intelligent, unselfish person makes the sacrifice without misgivings, eagerly anticipating the joy and fulfillment of parenting. In seeking spiritual growth, we must be ready to sacrifice many of the whims, bad habits, and indulgences craved by the personality, but the dedicated individual does it without regret, knowing that cooperation with the soul will lead to skills, joy, and states of being far beyond expectation. Far from involving the loss of anything, sacrifice leads us to new gains.

Nevertheless, people often demean the value of sacrifice. Selfish, exploitative individuals, for example, may consider it a sacrifice just to be considerate of others and treat them fairly. This is no sacrifice, however—just common decency! But such pseudo-sacrifice is commonly used by the exploiters of the world as a club to force others into agreement with their whims and demands. "Since I've agreed to treat you fairly," they suggest, "it's now up to you to sacrifice something, too, and do what I want." Such offers represent the direct opposite of cooperation and should never be accepted. Acting in the right way is *not* a sacrifice for anyone—even selfish, greedy people.

Nor should compromise be confused for sacrifice. Often in political or industrial negotiations, the two sides reach an impasse which can only be resolved by each side giving up goals it wanted. Compromise is reached—but it is not an act of cooperation! Neither side has really altered its selfishness. At the next bargaining session, the same demands are resurrected; the conflict reappears. The parties are just as uncooperative as ever.

A genuine sacrifice, by contrast, always leads to an increase in our cooperation with life. It causes us to reappraise our wishes and beliefs and see that some of them may not be as necessary or as vital as we have believed. In fact, when we compare them to what we will obtain by cooperating more fully, we decide that these old wishes and beliefs are actually detrimental to our best interests. So we unilaterally discard them, by changing our attitudes. We do not use them as *quid pro quo* in a bargaining session with the other parties concerned; we simply make a change within ourself. We discard the selfishness which has made us contentious.

It is through the practice of sacrifice that we discover the real potential of cooperation. The work of neutralizing our ignorance, laziness, and selfishness is indispensable, as it teaches us the basic lessons of cooperation and establishes the spirit of cooperating with life as a dominant theme in our character. But the practice of sacrifice takes us a step beyond, opening our character to the transcendent levels of cooperation. Guided by a deepening awareness of the soul and its destiny, we become more and more interested in serving life and helping to perfect it. As this change occurs, we come to realize that cooperation means a great deal more than just getting along well with others. It also includes:

Cooperating with ourself. We frequently sabotage our efforts by not cooperating with ourself. Sometimes, we even undermine the impact of our successes by refusing to honor them; we tell ourself we are not worthy of achievement. Cooperating with ourself, however, does not mean indulging our feelings or prejudices; it means aspiring to act in the right way and honor our potential—the nobility and goodness within us. We best cooperate with ourself by paying heed to our common sense, by listening to the voice of conscience within us, by seeking to grow, and by working in harmony with our duties and commitments.

Cooperating with our higher self. The personality has no enduring meaning or purpose unless it is cooperating with its senior partner, the soul. This is best achieved by striving to think as the soul would have us think, love as the soul would have us love, and act as the soul would have us act.

Cooperating with our plan for evolution—our destiny. Many people have no idea whither they are going or the purpose of their life. But as we learn to cooperate with life, we gradually discover that the soul has a carefully designed plan of growth for us, which is our destiny. By striving to cooperate with this plan, we prepare ourself to sense opportunities and new directions in life, and capitalize on them as fully as possible. We also develop the ability to see our weaknesses more clearly, so that we can take action to transform them into strengths of character. In addition, it is important to seek out a vision of our *future* potential for making a greater contribution to the human experience. This helps us discover our path to perfection and learn to pursue it.

Cooperating with universal order. Many of us maintain highly defensive and critical attitudes toward the laws of society, while professing a love for universal order. Part of learning to cooperate with the universe is to recognize that the laws of society—and our own personal conduct—are manifestations of the universal principles. Only by cooperating intelligently with the laws of society and the purposes they serve can we fully cooperate with universal order. Even more importantly, however, we need to increase our respect and reverence for such cosmic principles as the law of right human relationships, the law of cause and effect, the law of sacrifice, and the law of our inward parts—and honor them in our own acts and attitudes.

Cooperating with the unfoldment of the destiny of the whole of humanity. Like each individual, humanity as a whole is evolving and seeking fulfillment. The reservoir of human achievement is our culture and its offspring, civilization. We cooperate with human destiny by making our contribution to the enrichment of culture and civilization, through the arts, science, citizenship, or our generous support of worthwhile endeavors. The destiny of the collective effort of humanity is to harness the earth's resources so that all life forms, human and nonhuman, may evolve efficiently and completely.

Cooperating with groups and forces centered on the inner, invisible planes of life. There are numerous groups of enlightened beings, human and angelic, which operate from the inner planes. These entities seek intelligent and cooperative physical humans to work through, so that their creativity may have physical manifestation. These beings can be invoked by working creatively, by nurturing a deep sense of responsibility, by developing our skills and talents, and by living our life with a constant, full measure of goodwill. By aspiring to be a better person, we automatically draw the attention of such entities. And as we seek to serve humanity in unselfish, purely cooperative ways, it will become possible for these beings to work through us.

As we learn to cooperate in these ways, we begin to realize that it is possible to collaborate with life itself, to be a partner with God. This, in turn, gives us an appreciation of how our individual work fits meaningfully into the larger whole—the final masterpiece of creation to which we are all contributing.

A PARTNER WITH GOD

Cooperation enables us to achieve many things collectively which cannot be accomplished individually. A single violinist, no matter how virtuoso, cannot perform a symphony. Only an orchestra can. And an orchestra is not just a collection of talented individuals; it must be something greater. It must be a group of *cooperating* individuals, all uniting to perform a great symphony with harmony and beauty. The tympanist must suppress his egotistical desire to dominate all the other instruments, else he will ruin the performance. The violoncellist must be willing to pause when the music instructs him to rest and let the other instruments carry the symphony as written. The flutists cannot succumb to a fit of inertia or pique, failing to enter on cue. But more than that, the members of the orchestra must be willing to follow the direction and interpretation of the conductor, even when they disagree with it. They must cooperate with the basic principles of rhythm and pitch. They cannot decide to make up their own rules, playing in 6/8 time when the piece is written in 4/4, or retuning their instruments in some different way.

This kind of cooperation is part of the discipline of belonging to an orchestra. Its rewards come in the performance and ability of the orchestra to move and lift up the hearts of the audience. In our life, cooperation can have as much importance—if we build it, respect it, and use it as a tool in the art of living.

Cooperation is a tool which helps us evolve, an indispensable factor of growth. As we share what we have learned with others, we open new horizons for our development. And as we cooperate with our inner being—and the inner beings of others—we become more aware of our potential for evolving. New growth only becomes possible when we have demonstrated to the soul our capacity for dealing responsibly with what we have received in the past. Cooperation is a demonstration that we are using our opportunities responsibly.

Likewise, cooperation is a means for increasing productivity and satisfaction in our relationships and our careers. Selfishness and exploitation take so much energy to maintain that little strength remains for achieving anything worthwhile. As we learn to be cooperative, we find we can start channeling our energies into meaningful activities—and that people help us! This in turn opens up fresh opportunities which can never be realized by the uncooperative person.

Cooperation also is a means to greater effectiveness and efficiency in living. As we become more appreciative of the talents and contributions others can make, we see that we can coordinate our efforts with theirs more perfectly, benefiting everyone involved. We open new avenues for inspiration, support, and problem solving.

Above all, cooperation is a tool for living fully in the universe. As we learn about the nature of cooperation, we begin to appreciate more completely the fact that the universe has been cooperating with us all along. As long as we remain ignorant, we do not always understand the value of cooperation. As long as we are lazy, we do not always find it pleasant. As long as we cling to selfishness, we do not always welcome it. But as we give up our ignorant, lazy, and selfish ways, we discover that we really are an integral part of the universe and enjoy a marvelous relationship with it. If we cooperate with it, we will find it encourages us to develop our talents, consciousness, and humanity, so we can dwell more completely in the fullness of life.

Cooperation leads us to the discovery of brotherhood, the sharing of life with the rest of humanity. With brotherhood comes an awareness of three elements: communion, goodwill, and freedom. Communion is the union of all human souls and is a constant realization at the inner levels of life. Goodwill is a steadfast, benevolent regard for all others, coupled with a dedication to the fulfillment of the destiny of humanity. And freedom is the recognition that the selfishness, defensiveness, foolishness, and exploitation which entrap the personality are based on illusion. When we have entered the state of brotherhood by mastering cooperation, we are free from fear, free from manipulation by others, free from imposition, and free from harm or injury—because the universe works with us. We are free to grow and evolve as a unique and integral part of the kingdom of mankind.

As we begin to realize the value of brotherhood, we then also learn what it means to contribute to life. Part of this contribution, of course, is measured by the help we give others and the service we render to civilization. But our contribution goes far beyond this.

Whenever we touch others with love, we add to the strength and radiance of the energy of love as it flows through the world.

Whenever we act with intelligence, we enrich the power and light of intelligence within the universe.

Whenever we express nobility and dignity, we increase the presence of these qualities, not just in our life but in the whole of life.

Whenever we lift the hearts of others with joy, we add to universal joy.

Whenever we act with peace, we contribute to the spirit of peace which flows like a river.

It may not seem as though our individual, daily expressions of these qualities could make a significant contribution. But they do, just as every vote cast by a citizen in an election is of tremendous importance. Our individual efforts are as important as the efforts of the thousands of people who participated in landing a man on the moon. Without the competent and skilled contribution of *every* subcontractor involved in the project, the mission would have failed.

It is cooperation which gives our individual efforts great meaning. As long as we are self-centered, nothing we do is of importance. But as we dedicate ourself to cooperating with life, by expressing the life of God within us, the situation reverses; gradually, all that we do has enduring value.

And we become a partner with God.

THE MIND AND ITS USES

Its Nature and Purpose

The purpose of the mind is to lead us on voyages of discovery to brave new worlds. It is our tiny fragment of the Universal Mind; our key not only to making sense of our own life and circumstances, but to comprehending the mysteries and purposes of life itself.

A HERO'S STORY

The story of the unfoldment of human civilization is a saga of epic proportions: a tale of travail, triumphs, setbacks, discoveries, adventure, and ever-increasing advances. It is also the story of a hero, a hero who is often unsung—indeed, a hero who is frequently maligned by the foes of human development. To some, he is an unlikely hero; yet without his brave and noble efforts, the great civilizations of the past would never have materialized, our technological mastery of today would be unknown, and our hope for a better future would be nil. We would still be primitive savages disporting purposelessly in the wilderness.

This hero is the human mind. He is still largely untutored, because many of the members of humanity have not yet chosen to develop their portion of him. But in spite of this limitation, the accomplishments of the human mind on behalf of humanity have been nothing short of magnificent. By applying the mind to science, for example, we have partially understood and conquered the forces of nature, thereby enabling us to put these forces to work in supplying food for our sustenance, heat for our homes, and fuel for transportation. Similarly, by using the mind in engineering and architecture, we have been able to build homes which comfortably protect us from the elements, as well as other structures that let us gather together for work, relaxation, worship, government, education, and cultural inspiration. Thanks to the active use of the mind by inventors, we are blessed with airplanes that cross vast continents in hours, automobiles which give us a personal mobility inconceivable a hundred years ago, a tremendous array of appliances for use in the home, and the thousands upon thousands of industrial tools that have liberated us from the workaday drudgery of centuries past, opening to us new opportunities for developing greater competence and for finding deeper fulfillment in what we do. In the realm of medicine, the mind has uncovered ways of extending the span of life, as well as methods for reducing the discomfort of disease and pain. It has also been heroically at work in mankind's artistic expressiveness. While the artistic side of culture has often been considered more emotional than mental in orgin, the truth of the matter is different. The masterworks of Shakespeare, Rembrandt, Beethoven, da Vinci, Emerson, and their peers all bear the stamp of the artist who could *think* as well as express himself. The men and women who set the lasting standards of artistic excellence always are individuals who nobly express wisdom and intelligence. Indeed, it is no random fluke that the Golden Ages of artistic achievement coincide with periods in which the human mind flourishes on all fronts. In education, too, the mind excels: it is the mind which accumulates what we know about the world, the past, and human nature; it is the mind that preserves this knowledge and teaches it to succeeding generations, enabling civilization to endure and prosper. It is the mind which created the studies of psychology, philosophy, mathematics, astronomy, sociology, and history. Even in government, where rationality and logic so frequently seem overwhelmed by expediency and emotionalism, the mind has figured importantly. There has seldom been a finer representation of wisdom than in the group responsible for founding America—Jefferson, Franklin, Washington, Adams, Paine, Hamilton, and their colleagues.

Still, the role the mind has played in the advancement of human civilization is only half of the story. Equally important is the part the mind plays in the unfoldment of divine consciousness within each one of us individually. Many of us are unaware of this personal value of the mind, just as many of us pay small heed to the mind's contributions to culture. At best, we dimly sense the need to aspire to a "heaven within" (frequently misinterpreting it as a paradise apart), but have no idea that it is the *mind,* in its upper reaches, which constitutes this heaven. We are deeply impressed by accounts of miracles performed by people who appear to our glazed eyes as veritable superhumans, not realizing that the real miracle of human life is using the mind to think. And yet what a miracle thinking is! Without the mind, we would be dull-witted and animalistic, motivated only by our passions. But as the mind develops, a marvelous transformation occurs: we learn to register and use creative inspiration; we begin to comprehend our own nature, humanity, and purpose; we learn to relate intelligently to our environment; we discover how to take responsibility for our own care and development; we come to understand that we can be a proper steward for God's creation; and—most miraculously of all—we learn that we, too, can be co-creators with God and agents of universal justice.

Properly used, the mind leads us on to great discoveries, helping us grow in thought, emotion, and body. Furthermore, it gives us the means for analyzing and assessing the growth we make, so that it can become the seed for even greater development. And it lets us share these discoveries and evaluations with others—indeed, with the whole of humanity—so that they may benefit from our ideas, just as we have benefited from the ideas and inspirations of our forefathers.

It is absolutely vital that we steadily increase our ability to comprehend ourself and life—and equally important to apply what we know through our activities, attitudes, and creative contributions. Only in this way can the mind continue playing its part as hero; only in this fashion can the epic of human civilization proceed. When we fail to nurture and expand the mind, the possibility of transforming our life dims. When we are unwilling to discover and work with the fullness of the mind, the miracle of life fades. Our divine heritage remains unknown.

The wise and proper application of the mind is of incalculable importance to humanity, whether it is being used to discern the nature of life or capture inspiration and put it creatively to work. The successful outcome of the struggles of mankind depends upon the efforts of many people to cultivate the mind and use it constructively to reach noble goals; the successful outcome of our personal struggles depends on exactly the same thing.

As in all endeavors, however, more than just enthusiasm is needed to nurture and prepare the mind for intelligent use. A strong aspiration is important, of course, but it must be blended with an accurate understanding of how the mind works: its basic nature, plus the purposes and functions it has been designed to fulfill. Only when the nature and purpose of the mind are thoroughly comprehended does it become possible to perceive the correct means for developing and applying the mind to the affairs of living.

A study of the mind and the process of thinking is especially relevant at this stage of human unfoldment, when substantial numbers of people are capable of genuine mental activity—if they are properly guided and if they are willing to heed worthwhile direction. Learning to think in its fullest sense is not the simple matter we are led to believe it to be by our childhood mentors. It requires self-discipline, patient objectivity, and much dedicated work. But neither is it overly difficult. It is part of our human heritage to correctly develop the mind and master its uses. The rewards for the effort are greater discernment, knowledge, effectiveness, productivity, and fulfillment.

To succeed, we must let the "hero" within us arise and triumph.

THE FULL WHIR OF ACTIVITY

In beginning an assessment of the nature of the mind, it is best to distinguish between the mind itself and the outer garments it wears: the intellect and the physical brain. Materialistic thinkers needlessly confuse themselves and others by insisting that the mind is somehow crammed into the tiny cranial cavity which houses the human brain. Then, in the belief that they are dealing with the mind, they attach electrodes to the skull and chart the ebb and flow of brain waves reaching the outer surface of the head. Such "research" is no more helpful in understanding the process of thinking than tracking a symphony orchestra on an oscilloscope would be in understanding how composers write beautiful music.

Neither the mind nor the intellect is the same as the physical brain. They both operate *through* the brain at times, but their existence is independent of the physical brain, in a nonphysical dimension of thought. They also exist independently of each other. The mind is an important cognitive mechanism used by the soul or inner essence — a vehicle through which the soul gathers and processes knowledge. The intellect, by contrast, is the cognitive mechanism of the personality, and is therefore almost wholly composed of observations and associations made on the physical plane. Last and most definitely least, the brain is the instrument through which the mind or intellect can function physically.

Together, the mind, intellect, and physical brain form the human thinking apparatus. Their relationship to one another can perhaps be more clearly understood by comparing it to the reception of a television newscast. In order to receive the signal of the broadcast while sitting in our living room, we must have a television set. This television set corresponds to our physical brain, which is capable of receiving impulses from our intellect and mind. But just as it would be foolish to think that our television set itself gathers and prepares the news, and the commentators whose faces appear on the screen live within the set, it is likewise absurd to insist that our thoughts originate within the physical brain. They are merely registered there. The brain has no wisdom in its own right; it cannot interpret the impulses it receives, any more than the television set can explain why the weather is sunny instead of cloudy. Both the brain and the television merely relay to us impulses from other sources.

In the case of the television newscast, these impulses are the spoken words of the news commentator, converted into electromagnetic waves and broadcast from a central station. In the case of human thinking, the impulses received by the brain are the thoughts transmitted to it by the intellect. The intellect, then, is something like the news commentator working at the television studio. He takes the news and film clips which have been collected and generated by the vast reporting team working behind him, sorts and sifts them, and puts them in a reasonably organized format, with the important items first. He adds some continuity and polish, and then delivers the news on camera, so that we can see and hear it. Just so, the intellect is that portion of our mind which picks and chooses the information it deems applicable to our life and sends it to the physical brain, where we can become conscious of it. As might be expected, however, the quality of the information we receive from the intellect will depend on how well we have trained the intellect to operate, just as the quality of the newscast will depend upon the competence, skill, and objectivity of the anchorman.

The limitation of television newscasts, though, is that they can present only a tiny fraction of the news, in capsulate form. The intellect is limited in much the same way—but the mind is not. For the mind is something like the entire news gathering and writing staff of the television news department—its reporters, writers, directors, cameramen, and other personnel. They work behind the scenes and remain unseen to the camera's eye. And although the actual reports we eventually hear are heavily edited, the complete news is known to these professionals collectively. Just so, the mind is involved in everything which happens in the inner dimensions of thought, although its activities are often unknown to the physical brain. Even the intellect is frequently unaware of many of the mind's activities, especially at its higher levels.

Indeed, the intellect can be severely limited. Just as the anchorman may be more concerned about his personal appearance and the impact he makes on the audience than the quality of the news he delivers, so also the intellect can become absorbed in the trivial aspects of life on the physical plane and ignore the wisdom and inspiration of the mind. But in spite of these limitations of the intellect, the power and glory of the mind are not diminished. We must never confuse the inadequacies of the intellect with the magnificent potential of the whole mind.

In the average person who has not worked to develop his thinking ability, the mind is nonetheless at least fifty times greater in scope and power than the intellect. As an individual begins to train the mind, this ratio rapidly increases; when the mind is fully developed and enlightened, it is vastly greater than the intellect. At this point, the human mind literally knows no limitation except whatever limitations the mind of God has. *Indeed, the dimensions of the enlightened human mind are one and the same with the dimensions of the mind of God!*

In addition to placing the mind, intellect, and brain in their proper relationship, it is also important to distinguish between the processes of thinking with the mind and thinking with the emotions. In point of fact, the word "thinking" should only be used to refer to the use and activity of the mind. The proper word for describing the activity of the emotions is "emoting." Unfortunately, however, when people talk about thinking, they are usually referring to an emotional process, not a mental one. This error produces unnecessary confusion about the nature and function of the mind.

This confusion is sustained because it is fairly easy to appear to be thinking, when all along we are just reacting emotionally. It is possible, for example, to touch facts superficially with our emotions, become acquainted with those facts by forming opinions or beliefs about them, and then use them in such a way that we will fool others and ourself into believing we have actually thought about this data. In reality, though, all we have done is decide whether we like or dislike these facts, whether we should believe in them or not, and whether they should be avoided or pursued further. This creates the highly deceptive *illusion* of thinking.

True thinking, which brings the mind into play, goes much beyond merely touching the outer appearance of ideas, concepts, or facts with the emotions. It goes beyond the range of opinions, suppositions, and beliefs. Genuine thinking penetrates through the outer surface of an idea into its multidimensional interior, where it seeks to understand the nature, quality, intensity, purpose, origins, associations, and implications of the thought or fact. It digests the contents, qualities, and potency of the idea and thus converts the essence of the thought into a part of its own mental system.

Indeed, because the mature mind cherishes objectivity, it will dispassionately disregard any emotional reaction to ideas under consideration. It will shun the formulation of opinions, likes and dislikes, and the "belief structures" which form the *entire core of "thinking"* for so many people.

It is amazing how widespread emotional thinking is. Even the well-educated are often afflicted with it: many people "successfully" attend and are graduated from college without once engaging their *minds* in even a simple thought process. They bluff their way through with their knack for lightly touching facts with the superficial swish of their emotions. Others are so accustomed to substituting opinions and beliefs for real thinking that they resent and reject the genuine article when they encounter it. Yet few things are more frustrating to a mentally-awake person than having his carefully-prepared insights become the playthings of the emotionally mired. Asked to comment on a certain subject, for example, a thinking person will reply with an observation based on years of precise study and reflection, only to have the emotional pseudo-thinkers in the audience immediately protest: "But that's just your opinion!" And because they themselves cannot distinguish between bias and rationality, the pseudo-thinkers usually then conclude that the true thinking person is nothing but a prejudiced bigot.

Opinions and beliefs form no part of the thinking process – they are purely the result of emoting. The mind deals only with observable facts, their evaluation, and their application to life.

Fortunately, there is a fairly simple guideline for separating true thinking from the pseudo-thinking of the emotions. If, when someone says, "I think that such-and-such is true," he really means, "I *believe* that such-and-such is true," or "I would *like* such-and-such to be true," or "My prejudices *demand* that such-and-such be true," then he is not thinking at all. He is emoting. But if he means "I *know* such-and-such to be true because I have thoroughly researched it, evaluated it, and successfully applied it to life," then he is thinking. He is using his mind to deal with ideas.

It is important to understand and appreciate this distinction between thinking and emoting, because the vast majority of books written about the nature of thinking are really concerned with emoting. This problem is especially manifest in spiritual tracts which describe the mind as a "wild horse galloping in all directions" that must be stilled and reined in, lest it create havoc. Nothing could be farther from reality. It is the emotional nature, *not the mind,* which too often behaves wildly and must be stilled. Indeed, it is the mind that can tame the horse and ride it. Any efforts at stilling the mind will therefore make it all the more difficult to control the wild horse of the emotions. In fact, the price of stilling the mind is the death of any useful awareness.

Activity, not stillness, is the keynote of thinking. Whereas the emotions are much better off when calm and quiet, the mind is only really functioning when in the full whir of activity. Of course, we are not always aware of this activity, as it may occur on any one of a number of different levels — or on many levels simultaneously. When the mind is active consciously, we register its impulses in the brain as our moment-to-moment thoughts. But the mind can also be active subconsciously, in which case the brain is not impressed — and we are unaware of the thought currents at work "behind the scenes." The subconscious mind is composed of our memories, mental habits, and prefabricated associations; it is the support system upon which the intellect constantly relies for recollections and correlations. In addition, the mind can also be active supraconsciously. Such activity is seldom registered in the brain, however, because the supraconscious is independent of the personality. It existed before birth and will continue after death. The individualized portion of it contains the seeds of our basic character. The rest of it is the common mental heritage we share with all humanity and with God. The supraconscious serves as an immense reservoir of mental influences which subtly condition our thoughts and feelings, our unspoken words and actions.

The nature of thinking at these different levels varies greatly, both in intensity and quality. The conscious mind is easily distorted by the emotions and by excessive attention to the physical plane, and is limited to processing only a handful of different thoughts at the same time. (The theory advanced by some "experts" that the mind can only cope with *one* thought at a time is completely erroneous.) The subconscious mind, by comparison, can easily handle hundreds of thoughts at once, as it does when a specific thought triggers, by association, all related memories which have been stored since birth. But it can be distressingly narrow in its outlook and a major factor in resisting change and new growth. If left untended, the subconscious can quickly create a closed mind, in which all new information is systematically excluded or at least labeled "suspect."

Far greater than either the conscious or subconscious mind is the supraconscious. It can handle an infinite number of thoughts at the same time—which is one reason why so little of its activity is registered in the brain! And since it is relatively free of emotional and physical distortions, the quality of supraconscious thinking approaches pure objectivity. Much of it is a direct projection of the soul; it is therefore a valuable source of inspiration and guidance. But the visible signs of supraconscious thinking at work, shaping events, are usually rather subtle. If we make an important decision one day and the next day reverse it for the better, this may be an indication that the supraconscious mind has foreseen the unfortunate results of the original decision and canceled it in our best interests. Or, if we have an unconscious tendency to reject people who would mislead us, it may again be a sign of the supraconscious mind functioning as it should. Its influence may be so sublime, however, that we do not even perceive it. Our friends may notice it in our behavior, but we miss it unless they mention it to us. In both of these examples, the supraconscious influence is indirect; it filters into our actions and attitudes so quietly we usually do not observe it. And yet, it is nonetheless an active thinking process.

Thinking, then, could be operationally defined as the activity of the mind, whether conscious, subconscious, or supraconscious. But there are two other ways to define thinking as well, and each sheds a new light on the nature of the mind. Esoterically, the mind is considered the awareness mechanism used by the soul during incarnation. By implication, therefore, an esoteric definition of thinking would be the registration in the mind of impulses from many different dimensions, followed by the proper understanding and application of these observations to life. The impulses that the mind observes may come from the physical, emotional, or mental planes—or even higher ones—but true thinking only occurs when the impulses are interpreted and acted upon. If we are driving down the street, for example, and see a red blur above our head in front of us, it is not just enough to observe it and register it. We must correctly interpret it to be a red stop light, relate it to previous associations of red lights in the subconscious, and conclude that we must stop. Indeed, the cognitive process is only complete when we actually apply the brakes and bring the car to a halt. This example, of course, is an analogy which illustrates the component steps in thinking, rather than a description of the mind at work. Stopping for a red light is a trained, automatic physical response—it does not really bring the mind into play. Still, the same procedure can be applied to significant thinking situations. Perhaps we are insulted by a friend. The insult is an emotional impulse which in due course is perceived by the mind. If the mind is operating properly, it will first observe this emotional impulse objectively, to determine if it was intentional—or just a harmless statement our emotions have overblown. If we do find it was an intentional insult, the next step in the thinking process is to understand *why* this person offended us. There may be a variety of causes to consider: perhaps we offended him first, perhaps he is under great stress and behaving erratically, or perhaps he is simply an individual with a weak character who often acts immaturely. Having interpreted the incident as best we can, the final step is to draw appropriate conclusions and apply them to our life. If we find we offended him first, then obviously we must apologize for our insensitivity and forgive the insult. Or, if we realize he was under great stress or being immature, we take pity on him, extend our forgiveness, and help him see that there is a better way of acting.

The process of thinking can also be defined occultly, as the interaction of an individual mind (or a group of minds) with the entire plane of thoughts. We are not just limited to the thoughts generated within our own mind, after all; the miracle of thinking gives us access to an incredible storehouse of facts, information, ideas, patterns, and concepts. The mind is much more than the mere collection of memories and associations—even more than the mechanism for manipulating thoughts. It is a *body of intelligence* which far transcends the limitations of our physical senses, physical space, and time. In this occult sense, then, thinking is the act of focusing the attention on any desired information in the vast plane of thought and interacting with the quality of that data.

To fully understand the scope of thinking and the capacities of the mind, however, we must do more than just define the act of thinking. It is also necessary to comprehend the nature of the thoughts generated by the mind in action.

Metaphysically, a thought is the energy of an idea. This energy is not exhausted once the thought is formed; on the contrary, the process of focusing the thought converts latent energy into active power which can be usefully put to work. A thought can therefore be considered a seed for action—a seed either for more thinking, for emotional expression, or for physical activity. In this definition we can see the validity of the Biblical statement, "As a man thinketh, so is he." The nature of a person is determined by the kind of seed-thoughts he creates. We can also understand why thoughts and the mind can play such an important role in molding new attitudes and habits.

Psychologically, a thought is a *pattern* for habits, actions, concepts, attitudes, associations, or any manifest object. Without the patterns which result from thinking, there could be no coherent emotions, no organized physical existence, no habits, no attitudes—and certainly no philosophies or concepts. It is the thought pattern of architecture, for example, that gives a sense of structure to buildings—not the bricks or stones with which they are built. (Of course, it is important to understand that patterns of thought are not the same as the objects of thought. The idea or mental image of a sirloin steak is *not* identical to an actual sirloin steak sizzling on a plate in front of us!)

As we understand that thoughts are patterns, we come to recognize structured order as a basic characteristic of consciousness. To think is to give order and structure to whatever it is we are thinking about. Moreover, by thinking we can find order in anything which confuses us — *because the potential order already exists as a fundamental characteristic of thought.*

Philosophically, a thought is defined as a child of mind that is infused with a portion of our real life. It is not just a meaningless figment or chemical reaction of the brain; rather, it is a living thing, a part of our life. Every thought formed in our mind is an expression of our humanity — good, bad, or indifferent. And because our thoughts are children of the mind, they can grow up and reproduce themselves — they engender consequences, good, bad, or indifferent. Thus, we have a responsibility — to our own best interests, to others, and to all humanity — to be careful how we think and direct our thoughts. Our thoughts can be powerful, because we impart a portion of our livingness to them. If we are careless, foolish, or malicious, our thoughts can be destructive; they can corrupt and poison, and turn on us like vindictive children turning on their parents. But if we are rightly motivated, unselfish, and wise, our thoughts will be constructive; they will be the tools with which we discover the heaven within — and build a heaven on earth.

Occultly, a thought is a combination of substance and movement — a vibration or subtle sound. The *substance* of thought is the exceedingly rarefied matter of the mental plane — but that alone is not a thought. Nor is the occult term "thoughtform" exactly the same as a thought; it is only the clothing of the thought. A thought is the vibratory *movement* of mental substance. The nature and intensity of this vibration determines the quality and significance of the thought.

The movement of a thought can be of two kinds—that which is internal to the substance of the thought, plus the movement of the thoughtform as a whole. In other words, the motion of a thought can be like the movement in a human being: there can be internal movements, such as the beating of the heart, as well as movements of the whole form, such as running. Great significance lies in this fact. The average human thinker is only interested in the external movement of the thought—what he himself provides through the impetus of the act of thinking. But the careful, disciplined thinker will also pay heed to the internal qualities of the thought, thereby learning the full dynamic potential of the mental energy at his disposal.

Each of these approaches to thought instructs us as to its nature. A thought is a living body of intelligence, shaped by the activity of the thinker into a pattern of order and purpose which carries with it the seed of action. The total of all thoughts within the universe forms the plane of thoughts or mental plane. The sum of all our thoughts—conscious, subconscious, and supraconscious—forms our individual mind.

In some of us, this is not saying a lot. The size and development of human minds covers a vast spectrum, from very primitive to quite extraordinary. These differences are more dramatic than they might at first appear. To state that there is disparity among human minds is not like saying there are differences in human appearance—some people being plain or ugly, others being ravishingly beautiful; some being short, some tall; some being black, others white, brown, yellow, or red. It is more like stating that the physical bodies of the first animal-man, which appeared millions of years ago, would be *scarcely recognizable* if placed alongside of the typical physical body of modern man. And indeed, the mind of an illiterate bears almost no similarity to the enlightened mind of a Thomas Jefferson, a Buddha, a Nikola Tesla, or a Christ.

Why is there such a great disparity in human minds? The answer is simple: enlightened people have educated, trained, nurtured, and applied their minds. Stupid people have not. It is not because Providence has decreed that some people will be blessed with great mental prowess and others will be dull-witted — the potential for developing the mind is the same for all. But the mind does not grow automatically; it requires active encouragement. It is a body — a body of thoughts — which can grow like the physical body. Unlike the physical body, however, it does not grow all by itself. We have reached a stage in human development in which the physical body will grow to adulthood without active encouragement, as long as it is fed and not excessively abused. But an infant mind will remain an infant forever unless it is deliberately educated and used. People do not become educated simply by spending twelve years in a classroom; nor do they necessarily become wiser as they grow older, in spite of popular myths that they do. Usually, they become more entrenched in their unthinking ways.

Since the mind has been designed for active use, it will develop only when stimulated by practical use. But it must be exercised according to its design, or it will not mature properly. It will therefore be helpful to know how the mind is intended to operate.

The mind operates by observing incoming impulses carefully, analyzing these observations and sorting them into meaningful groupings, finding parallels, correspondences, and associations within these groups, and relating the new information to data that has already been processed, understood, and stored in the subconscious. As it goes through these steps, the mind gradually knits together this massive amount of input into a framework which reveals the basic order of the thoughts, touching other points of reference already understood to some degree. In due course, this inherent order emerges into clarity, until the interpretation of the new information becomes obvious and unquestioned. *Until this inherent order or meaning is completely obvious to the conscious mind of the thinker, the thinking process is not complete.*

Through a sufficiently developed mind, we gain entrance to the plane of thoughts — also known as the mental plane — and the privilege to work at that level. Indeed, this is the foremost value of learning to think — that it enables us to operate on the mental plane and relate to its qualities, possibilities, and riches. Since the mental plane is actually a reflection of the mind of God, a tremendous abundance of wisdom, insight, creative inspiration, comprehension, and discernment can be ours for the asking.

The mental plane is not at all like the astral plane, or plane of emotions. Because the astral is a plane of force, our experiences at that level are largely shaped by our own individuality — our prejudices, likes and dislikes, and wants and wishes. Everything is relative in dealing with the emotions, and therefore unreal, unless grounded in the purpose of the inner being. Astral energies are extremely elastic and pliable — ever-changing, subjective. The mental plane, by contrast, is a plane of form, not force. As a result, it has an objective existence independent of our individuality or our own perception of it, just as the physical world has an objective, independent existence unaffected by our physical presence or absence. The reality of the mental plane is not relative or dependent upon our personal whim; it is orderly, stable, and absolute. The concept of beauty as set forth in the mind of God, for example, cannot be changed by our personal desires. It is an absolute which can be observed, appreciated, contacted, and used—but we serve it, it does not serve us. Consequently, if our perceptions of the mental plane are to be accurate, objective observation is crucial. Imposing a personal interpretation or bias upon what we observe mentally will distort those observations—the degree of distortion depending upon our background, intentions, and motivation. While pure objectivity may seem to be an impossible goal to some, it is actually not so hard to attain—if we are willing to work mentally and subdue the emotional tendency to discolor and give everything a personal, prejudiced slant. With proper training, the mind is able to see with great clarity, because the substance, laws, and qualities of the mental plane are *not* subject to the confusion and bewilderment so common to the astral.

The forms on the mental plane are not exactly the same as the forms on the physical plane, of course. But neither are they radically different. It might be said that the forms on both of these planes *correspond* to each other. Mental forms are the subtle patterns from which physical forms are created—be they objects, events, conditions, skills, habits, or relationships. Thus, mental forms could be called the "blueprints" for physical forms and functions. In other words, the idea of a chair in the mind of a craftsman is the pattern from which the physical chair is ultimately built. The idea of a fine gourmet meal is the pattern that gives a cook direction and focus for seeking out appropriate recipes, buying foodstuff, and preparing the actual meal. The idea that a certain service can be performed to fill a consumer need is the blueprint from which a successful business can be created.

It must be understood, however, that a mental form has a number of different components, each made of a specific quality of mental substance. Usually, these components are lumped into two categories: the concrete attributes of thought and the abstract aspects of thought. The concrete portion of a thought would be the specific details of the blueprint: its facts, applications, and structure. By comparison, the abstract portion would be the *essence* of the blueprint: its qualities, purposes, and sublime nature. In the mental blueprint or pattern of a chair, for instance, such concepts as the proportions of the various parts, the basic design, and the fact that it can be used for sitting would all be ingredients in the concrete thought. The abstract portion of the thought would be the idea of "chairness"—the archetypal patterns of supportiveness, comfort, and usefulness.

The novice in the realms of the mind is able to contact only the concrete levels of thought and must be careful not to make the mistake of assuming that these outer attributes are the entire content of a thought. Without its inner, abstract essence, a thought is a hollow shell, lacking in force and purpose, and relatively meaningless. Nonetheless, due to the elusive, sublime nature of abstract thoughts, the novice often wonders what their role in the thinking process really is. This can perhaps be best explained by examining the thought sequence involved in creative work.

A true creative worker begins at the abstract level, with the observation of an emanation of God's plan and divine ideals, followed by the decision to create something on the physical level which captures and expresses the essence of that archetype. In preparing a gourmet meal, for instance, a creative cook would start with a basic perception that certain ingredients could be skillfully combined to produce a marvelous new taste treat, instead of beginning with a recipe invented by someone else and culled from a cookbook. This perception would be an abstract thought, capturing the essence of taste and nutrition. As the abstract idea takes shape in the mind, it is then projected into the concrete levels of thinking, where it becomes more specific and acquires definite attributes. In other words, the cook begins formulating the specific ingredients to be used, the proper amounts of each, how they should be processed or cooked, and similar details. The creative process is completed when the concrete pattern is actually used to produce the desired physical reality: the gourmet delight.

There are notable differences between the concrete and abstract portions of thought. Whereas perception of the concrete attributes is basically a question of seeing what is there, the perception of an abstract aspect is more like seeing everything within the thought. It is *in*sight, to use that word in its literal meaning. True perception of an abstract idea would be more like receiving the insight of how to prepare fifty different gourmet dishes from a single principle than merely being inspired with a single entree. The ability to think abstractly is the capacity to comprehend perfectly the esoteric significance and practical value of any subject—even if very few of the details of that subject are consciously known.

A powerful example of the nature of abstract perception is an instance from the life of Nikola Tesla, the electrical genius who made practical the use of alternating current systems for generating and transferring electricity. In a short period of time on a winter afternoon in a park in Budapest in 1882, Tesla received a flash of insight which enabled him to solve the problems of generating alternating current, which the electrical experts of his day considered unsolvable — and also gave him the basis for many of his subsequent inventions. What Tesla perceived during that experience was not the concrete details of how alternating current would work, but the basic principles of electricity. In that moment, *he comprehended electricity!* It was then a relatively simple matter, since he was highly trained in the field, to work out the details of how to apply the essential principle.

There is an infinite variety of these mental forms, these abstract/concrete blueprints, which we can summon to us through the mind and put to work in our life. We summon them by training the mind and by having a purposeful intention to comprehend some aspect of life. But as we go about the business of invoking these mental forms, it is a good idea to remember that they are far more subtle than any forms we have dealt with before. On the physical and astral levels, forms can be readily perceived by their shape, size, opacity, and color. Not so on the mental level: here the forms are more like the images on the graphic display unit of a computer, although this is only an inadequate analogy. Computer-created images are more geometrical than solid and can be rotated through three dimensions on the display screen. making it possible to study them from any angle. In much the same way, mental forms are primarily geometrical; however, instead of three dimensions, they "rotate" through five dimensions. When we are operating in complete awareness on the mental plane, it seems as though we are being bombarded by mental forms coming at us in all directions, and that each of these forms is itself a point or axis around which myriad other mental forms orbit.

What we actually perceive on the mental plane is movement, direction, function, structure, impulse, and order, rather than shape, size, opacity, and color. For a novice, however, it requires a lot of patient retraining to start registering these mental characteristics, since we are accustomed to making physical and astral observations, which are different. And so, for a long time, our subconscious—in its effort to please us—automatically translates the pure mental imagery into the more traditional forms we have grown up observing. This does let us deal with mental forms more readily, but it also distorts them to a certain degree. It brings in our personal associations and reduces our objectivity.

Indeed, most published descriptions of the mental plane and its forms are actually based on perceptions made from the astral level, rather than directly on the plane of thoughts. As a result, these accounts contain built-in distortions which must be weighed by anyone seeking objective understanding.

In understanding the nature of the mental plane, it is also important to comprehend how mental forms are created—and who creates them. Abstract mental forms are created by divine cognition. Then, as creative thinkers interact with these abstract forms, they sharpen their specificity (*not* their clarity or definition) and thereby produce concrete forms. Next, as they and others deal with these concretized forms, still other ideas, concepts, facts, and theories are created. Many of these concepts and theories are useful, but not all of them; at this level distortion and contamination can enter. Indeed, a certain amount of pollution does exist on the lower levels of the plane of thoughts. However, it has all been generated by humans — by misinterpreting facts, succumbing to illusions, and trying to personalize ideas. The abstract levels of the mental plane are free of that kind of distortion. And even the concrete levels have only a minor amount, when compared to the sickening pollution of the astral plane.

This last point needs emphasizing. The hallmark of the mental plane is that it is a plane of intelligence, ideas, and knowing. It is a place where objective understanding can be achieved, free from any interference from the emotions. Nothing obscures the proper observation and comprehension more than strong desires, fears, worries, and personal whims. There are no such elements on the plane of thoughts, however. And so, it is the ideal place for achieving the detachment and poise needed for accurate analysis and evaluation of thoughts. In addition, since it is a plane of form and does not have the elasticity of the astral, the mental plane is a place where we can achieve stability — a stability rooted in knowing who we are, what we are designed to do, and how to do it. Stabilized at this level, we can more easily focus on our purpose, principles, values, and inner essence. These elements in turn create an even greater equilibrium of consciousness.

Stability and equilibrium should not be confused with stillness and silence, however. These are *not* characteristics of either the mental plane or the enlightened mind. In fact, to impose stillness or silence on the mind is unnatural and undesirable. The normal state of the mental plane and the individual mind is controlled, regulated, and orderly activity. Only the emotions need to be stilled and calmed, to keep them from interfering with the workings of the mind. The emotions are something like a body of water, which can be whipped into squalls and high waves. This turbulence can interfere with the life of the people on shore, distracting them from their normal activities during the period of storm and flooding. The mind can also be adversely affected by emotional pressures, if they are not controlled and kept calm. But the normal condition of the mind is to be busy with creative and responsible work and activity. The enlightened person uses the stability of the mind as a safeguard against emotional disturbance, thereby protecting his active involvement in life from interruption.

In fact, as we explore the realm of the mind we gradually come to understand that the mental plane is the real focus of human endeavor—much more so than either the physical or emotional planes. It is here we encounter, for the first time, human *life;* on the physical and emotional levels we merely encounter the *manifestations* of human life. It is here that genuine growth and renewal can occur; it is here that we can understand one another; it is here that we commune. It is at this mental level that we set in motion all of the significant events of physical life and all of the meaningful expressions of our emotional nature.

To complete the analogy comparing the emotions to a lake of water, the physical body can be likened to the bottom of the lake—very much influenced by the water above it but with a reality of its own, providing a base for underwater plants, a home for marine animals, and so on. The mind, then, corresponds to a person living on shore, *above* the water. Such a person can see his reflection in the water, and can even see that life at the bottom of the lake is not so dissimilar from life on dry ground. But the life at the bottom is only a poor copy of life on shore, with fewer creative opportunities and less potential for use. And so, while the person from time to time swims in the lake and dives to the bottom, he chooses to live above water, on dry ground, where he can see more clearly. This is where his *real life* is, where he can lead a full and active life. On dry land, he is free to travel about, visiting other people, working, and discovering the many facets of life. He can even fly up into the air and be totally removed from the water and its bottom.

No analogy is perfect, but this one does demonstrate the relative value of the mind. To live with an undeveloped mind is like living, trapped, at the bottom of a lake, constantly at the mercy of the water's currents. Having a keen and well-trained mind, by contrast, is like having free access to the entire world and all its riches, for the mind is the center of our real life.

But the value of having a fully enlightened mind is more than just being able to operate in the entire plane of thoughts. The enlightened mind is also the connecting link between the soul and the personality. At its abstract levels, the mind is in direct contact with the soul, our immortal essence. It is meant to function as our awareness mechanism for the spiritual impulses of will, wisdom, and love, as well as to serve as the thinker, director, and organizer of the personality.

Until the mind is properly trained and able to operate freely on the mental plane, however, the soul cannot use the personality directly for its work. Thus, both the soul and the personality are hobbled by an immature, untrained mind. The immature mind is ignorant and unable to discern what it needs to perceive; it is incapable of making sense of what has been perceived. Just as a small child can starve to death in the midst of a well-stocked pantry, because it has not yet learned to recognize food and prepare it, an immature mind can be the cause of spiritual starvation.

As we enlighten the mind, it enriches our life. Training the mind automatically opens the way for new opportunities, horizons, and interests. It nurtures a growing awareness that we do possess the power to operate above our struggles and the hardships of physical and emotional turmoil. Eventually, it gives us a sense of constantly living in the presence of our inner greatness, the soul.

This, then, is the nature of the mature mind: that it is the stairway to the presence of our soul—the stairway to the heaven within us.

SERVANT OF THE SOUL

To understand the purpose of the human mind, a basic assumption must be made: that the mind is a servant of the soul. If the mind is thought of independently from the soul, it has no purpose. A function, yes, but not a purpose. In such a condition, it could only be an immature mind—unfulfilled and unrealized, directed only by the whim of the emotions.

Of course, all elements of the personality are designed to be servants of the soul. But the mind has the added distinction of being designed to be the *direct agent* of the soul in the affairs of the personality, something like a foreman supervising the activities of the other workers. And the soul bestows upon the enlightened mind full authority to be the master of the personality, to discipline and direct the emotions and the physical body as required. In truth, the mind in its fullness is much closer to the soul than it is to the lower elements of the personality. It constantly consults with the soul as it goes about its business of supervising the activities of the personality, seeking help, inspiration, and guidance.

The mind fulfills this role as supervisor of the affairs of the personality on an ongoing basis, whether we are consciously aware of it or not. Highly evolved individuals consciously participate with their minds in this work; the rest of humanity perform it primarily at the supraconscious level and therefore have no waking recollection of it. Of course, in some individuals, the work is thwarted; the emotions or physical urges rebel against the supervision of the mind and soul. They ignore self-discipline, scoff at the need for ethical behavior, and follow the carrot of their own selfishness. As a general rule, however, such rebellion can only occur when the mind is too immature and weak to fulfill its purpose. The emotional-physical insurrection can be quelled if the mind is trained to operate in its fullness.

It is important to realize that in executing its authority as supervisor and master of the personality, the mind does not use its own power. Thoughts do have power of their own, but the potency used by the mind in regulating the personality emanates originally from within the soul. In this way, the mind is again like a television set, which contains no substantial power of its own. It is animated by electricity and inspired by the signal broadcast from the television studio. Just so, the mind is animated by the life force flowing from the soul and inspired by the light of the soul. It has to be trained over a long period of time to freely accept this life force and respond clearly and correctly to its light.

As part of its function as the supervisor of the personality, the mind is designed to manipulate the life force which enters the mind, emotions, or physical body, and thereby construct specific thoughts, feelings, conditions of health, or physical events in line with the soul's chosen plan. In this way, it can direct the activities of the personality toward acquiring certain skills, modifying undesirable habits, and altering the focus of its attention.

A second major purpose of the mind is to assimilate and digest mental food and nourishment. This activity is much like the physical process of eating food, digesting it through enzyme action in the stomach and intestines, absorbing it into the blood, and carrying it through the circulation to the cells, where it is used to power the muscles, repair tissue, and perform other activities. The mind, however, eats ideas, not food. It digests them by discerning their particular value and relevance and then assimilates them by associating them with other ideas and memories in the subconscious. Having done that, it completes its work by focusing the power of the digested ideas into the varied aspects of our life, where it can go to work and be productive.

Digesting mental food is not as automatic as its physical correlate, however. It requires active, conscious involvement. Unfortunately, far too many of us gulp down our ideas whole, without chewing them, breaking them down, or assimilating them. They remain undigested in the subconscious. From time to time these stored ideas are recycled and thought about, but this activity is more like chewing our cud than actually thinking. It gives us the illusion of absorbing new ideas, but has no nutritive value.

Since one of the mind's functions is to digest ideas, it should be obvious that we must be discriminating in choosing the kind of mental food we consume. It is alarming how many people are not. Some people will swallow anything, without considering the possible harmful effects; others develop a taste for mental junk food – presweetened ideas, hot dog concepts, and pop pablum. These people gorge themselves on such "treats," not realizing they are all starch and no protein. Enlightened people, however, partake of more solid food, selected from the cornucopia of the higher mind.

The mind also serves as an integrative force within the personality. Its role in this regard is multifaceted. The immediate goal of integration for most people is to draw together the elements and forces of the personality and unite them in a cohesive whole. But once this level of integration has been achieved, the need for additional work arises: integration of the intellect with the intuition, the concrete with the abstract portions of thought, the knowledge we have gained with our potential for wisdom, and – above all – the personality with the soul.

The mind is effective in this work of integration because it operates by finding the inherent order of things. The process of integration always begins by determining what various events or facts mean and interpreting how they relate to us – by making sense of the world around us. We take inventory of the contents of our mind, consciously and subconsciously, and assess the value of our activities, attitudes, and motives. As we discover aspects of the personality which are too harmful to be assimilated into the ultimate whole, we "integrate" them by dissolving or eliminating them, thereby purifying the personality. In this way, we act like an all-consuming fire, which integrates with trash by burning it. The mind has great power for this, for as it discovers aspects of the personality which are not cooperating with the inherent order of our life, it will smash through them and break them up, be they stereotypes, distortions, illusions, self-deceptions, or erroneous assumptions.

At the same time, whenever the mind finds that elements of the personality are missing which ought to be present—skills, insights, self-awareness, the capacity to love, and qualities of consciousness—it "integrates" by building the necessary skills and dimensions. No part of the personality but the mind has the capacity to work in this manner. And only the enlightened mind is able to build these new dimensions of personality in harmony with the divine ideals of the soul.

When the work of purification and building is finished, the process of integration stands completed. The diverse parts have been harmonized; order has been generated where confusion and chaos once reigned. It is the soul which determines what the finished product shall be, but it is the mind—the part of our consciousness which links our higher and lower selves—that carries out the actual work.

Of all the purposes of the mind, however, the most significant is that the mind has been designed to be an explorer—a discoverer which conquers new horizons of consciousness and understanding by breaking through limitations and expanding the sphere of its involvement in life. The mind has been infused with the spirit of discovery, and once we learn to harness and direct it, the mind becomes a remarkable channel for growth and development.

The characteristic of the immature mind and the pseudo thinker is to impose limitations, by being closed-minded, prejudiced, fearful, doubting, and uninterested in anything except selfish concerns. Such a person remains trapped in his self-constructed prison walls until he realizes that the real potential of the mind lies in exploring and conquering new mental territory—the invisible dimensions and uncharted regions of the plane of thoughts.

In fulfilling this role of the mind, we must be like the ancient explorers and discoverers of "new" worlds—people such as Magellan, Columbus, and Marco Polo. These were brave, courageous individuals who left the limited, bounded societies of medieval Europe and voyaged to unknown lands—the Americas, the South Seas, and China. They discovered new countries and cultures and brought back to Europe artifacts, riches, ideas, and even inhabitants of these distant continents. In so doing, they immeasurably enriched the life and society of western Europe, and were an important factor in the dawning of the Renaissance. From China they brought many ideas and ways of living which were immediately incorporated into the civilization. From the Americas they brought back new plants, food, and animals—and a stupendous amount of wealth.

The Magellans, Columbuses, and Marco Polos of humanity do not just go sailing around the world, however, taking a scenic tour. They *discover* new lands, not only in the sense of finding them for the first time but also in the sense of finding what is unique and valuable about them, and how the essence of the discovery can be brought back and incorporated into their own lives, their own society. Their lives are triumphs of will and nerve over the inertia of the average person, and their acts of discovery are inspirations to the rest of us. For just as the accomplishments of such individuals are heroic, so also can our minds be heroic—if we pursue the spirit of discovery.

To each of us is open the vast panorama of the mental plane, filled with its diverse ideas, patterns, thoughts, concepts, and directions. Yet the mental plane, while well-known to the advanced thinkers of humanity, nevertheless remains all but uncharted and unexplored by the vast majority. Indeed, there are scarcely any books in print which do more than suggest that the realms of the mind are there, waiting to be conquered.

That is not enough! Like Columbus and Magellan, we must build up our own mind so that it becomes a noble vessel in consciousness, and then sail forth to explore the realm of the mind and what it offers. But even this will not suffice; to discover the mental plane in its fullest, we will have to bring back what we find to be of value—the artifacts, riches, ideas, and realizations which can be incorporated beneficially into daily life. And we must share our discoveries with others and use them to enrich society.

Such discoveries can truly lead to a renaissance in our life. The power of the human mind in revealing the larger dimensions of the art of living has been demonstrated repeatedly in the lives of all great human explorers of consciousness. Our inspired religious teachers and prophets have been explorers of the hidden dimensions in the mind of God. Our outstanding scientists have been fearless probers in the "raincloud of knowable things." Our leading psychics and occultists have been dauntless explorers on the mental and spiritual planes. All these adventurers, be it a Ralph Waldo Emerson, Edgar Cayce, Nikola Tesla, H.P. Blavatsky, Ramakrishna, St. Theresa, or St. Paul, have tapped new mental territory, brought back new mental treasures and insights, and have greatly enriched our lives. We can do the same. *In fact, we have been designed to do the same!*

The mind is the visionary element of the personality, able to see to the farthest horizon and beyond it. It blends together the functions of the five physical senses and then transcends them, creating a "super sense" of great significance. Unlike the five physical senses, the super sense of the mind, when trained, can achieve true objectivity and perfect accuracy. Moreover, it can be much more versatile than the physical senses, able to pierce the outer shell and distortions of any aspect of life and find the truth within it.

Truly, the enlightened mind is a marvel. Where pseudo-thinkers place limitations and say "stop," the enlightened mind penetrates and proceeds. Where the small intellects and doubters say "impossible," the enlightened mind discovers a way to do it. Where the ignorant proclaim that nothing exists, the enlightened mind boldly sallies forth and finds God in His fullness. And where nihilists insist that there is no meaning, the enlightened mind not only discovers but also demonstrates purpose.

THE GREATEST DISCOVERY

We have a choice, then: to continue to indulge an immature, untrained mind, or to nurture our mind so that it can become the agent of the soul, the discoverer of new worlds. We may not wish to be responsible for our mind and our thoughts, but the universe does hold us accountable, regardless of our reluctance.

Our mind is a living part of our humanity; we must therefore be careful how we think and direct our thoughts. Every time we create a thought, we pour a measure of our livingness into it. We create a child of thought. Whereas physically we may father or give birth only to a few children, or none at all, in our mental life we produce tens of thousands of thought offspring. Some of them are cruel little creatures, nasty and mean bastards we would prefer to disown. But by practicing the principles of planned mental parenthood, there is no reason why our thought children cannot be noble, loving creations which honor us and give us cause to be proud.

In this simple formula is set forth all any of us needs to know about attaining heaven. If our thought children are cruel and nasty, we will soon find ourself in a hell on earth. But if our creations are pure and noble, they will reveal to us the secret of the heaven within.

Many people believe — as the result of pseudo-thinking — that heaven is a place which can only be reached after we die, and then only by people who believe they are deserving enough to be admitted. In point of fact, the true heaven worlds are on the mental plane and are reached by learning to operate at those levels. Only the adventurous at heart, the skilled in thinking, and the pure of consciousness can enter these realms — but we all have the equipment and the opportunity to do just that. And there is no point in waiting until we die; heaven can be attained at any time!

This, of course, is the greatest discovery of all: that through the development and use of an active mind we can find heaven and bring heaven to earth. The active, enlightened mind links us with the powers and forces of heaven, enables us to focus and concentrate them, and allows us to express a heavenly consciousness in all we do. Making this link is important not just to each of us individually; it is of profound importance to the whole human race, to all of civilization, and to God.

Because the mental plane reflects the mind of God,

we can find God by developing our mind—much more so, in fact, than by developing our heart, although this is important, too. *And God can find us!* Immature minds are of little value to God, but God does use the enlightened minds of the human race as His best vehicle for projecting spiritual impulse and light into the earth plane. It is the destiny and purpose of each one of us to participate in this work, and the sooner we can prepare for it, the better. It is no longer enough to sit back and expect that a rare teacher or saint here and there will be enough to satisfy the needs of God. The potential exists *now* for the organized and enlightened minds of the world to form a network through which God can disseminate His light and wisdom.

To be sure, it is work which demands heroes. But through the proper cultivation and use of the mind, ordinary people can indeed become heroes. *We can all become heroes,* by recognizing our destiny and fulfilling it. And by becoming builders of a noble consciousness, a noble life, and a noble civilization, we can all help God fulfill His exalted destiny as well.

THE MIND AND ITS USES

Its Development and Application

The mind is like a lens through which the light of the soul can be focused into the personality. As we learn to "cut and polish" the lens of the mind, it becomes increasingly useful to us — and the inner self. Through the mind, we not only can *find* the inner self, but also come to *know* its nature and its ways.

THE LENS OF THE SOUL

Each human life is potentially a voyage of discovery, a journey to the farthest reaches of our personal world—and beyond. For a long time, we remain unaware of this noble potential; we may occasionally sally forth on brief expeditions, but mostly, our fears and inertia hold us back from any serious investigation into life. Timidly, we stay at home and take care not to ask questions, lest they kindle an interest that will force us to look for answers. In this way, we become entrenched in our own private "dark age" resisting the attempts of our inner essence to inaugurate a renaissance. Nevertheless, there does come a time when we begin to understand that deep within us is a powerful force which yearns to conquer the unknown, seeks to define more clearly who we are and what we can do, and strives to honor and fulfill the purposes of God. Gradually, we realize that the journey of self-discovery is a noble one, and we decide—at last!—to embark upon it.

This journey takes us across the length and breadth of human experience. We visit the continents of activity, creativity, and achievement; we sail the oceans of self-doubt. We climb the mountains of aspiration and struggle through the desert sands of setback and seeming failure. With every step, we acquire new skills, understanding, stature, and confidence. We encounter moments of pleasure and excitement, danger and triumph, but they all lead us onward to our goal — if we are willing to learn from them. For on this journey, all roads lead to self-discovery.

There are two ways to approach this voyage within. We can set out impulsively, taking with us only our enthusiasm, hopes, and our good intentions. This would be like setting out on a journey up the Amazon with one change of clothes, a couple of sandwiches, a pen knife, and a credit card — expecting to stop at motels every night! With such superficial preparation, our trip would be a disaster. The alternative, of course, is to plan the journey in advance, gather the needed supplies, and acquire the skills and knowledge which will help us survive the rigors of the trip, reach our goal, and return safely. For such a rugged trip as traveling up the Amazon, we would have to master the skills of handling a boat, surviving in the wilderness, identifying edible wild plants, and speaking Portuguese. On a voyage of self-discovery, we would need mental skills: the abilities to think logically and perceptively, to make sense of new situations, and to find the proper way.

Obviously, this second method of preparing for the journey is vastly superior to the first. It is the mind which makes the difference, not merely good intentions; it is the ability to think clearly and thoroughly that spells success, not enthusiasm alone. *Indeed, an active, mature mind is one of the greatest assets we can take on our journey of self-discovery.* In making this expedition, there is a constant need for learning new skills, making intelligent decisions, and applying our talents in practical ways. Without the mind, this is virtually impossible. Without the mind, we are likely to wander off course into pits of quicksand. Without the mind, we are constant prey for the "wolves in sheep's clothing" who would attack us. In fact, without the mind, we are just as apt to start looking for the Amazon in China or India as in South America.

The mind has been specifically designed to be used on this voyage of self-discovery. Properly trained, it is the ideal tool for comprehending our nature, our relationship to God, and our place and importance within the universe; for establishing order in life and increasing our competence; and for properly discerning the noble elements of life and effectively expressing them in all we do.

But the mind must be carefully cultivated. Many people assume that the mind develops naturally as we grow older, but it does not; unless specifically educated, it remains an uncoordinated infant, even while the physical body matures. Nor does a commitment to spiritual living automatically mean the mind will grow, like flames bursting to life in a fireplace the moment we decide, "Let's have a fire." It takes work to build a fire: we must gather wood, lay it properly, light it, and then fan the flames. Even then, more wood must be regularly added to the fire, or it will soon die. It is much the same with developing the mind: we begin by gathering facts, knowledge, and ideas from many sources; then we must assemble this input correctly, so that it can be ignited with a spark of comprehension; finally, we must keep our mental "fire" burning with curiosity and skillful application.

A mind which can function in these ways will be most helpful in our voyage of self-discovery. It will be able to perceive where we are headed and the purpose we are fulfilling. On the strength of such insights, it will then be able to wisely prepare for a successful journey. It will know what skills to develop, the strengths of human character to emphasize, which "languages" of intuition to learn, the supplies from the universal storehouse to stock, and which companions to travel with.

Unfortunately, many people who would like to use the mind effectively in life have done very little to train it. They may know that the mind has been designed for noble use, but they have not yet put this understanding to work. Perhaps they have had the misfortune to be taught — as is so common today — that the mind is actually harmful and should therefore be used as little as possible. Such a notion is antihuman and degrading, but it can understandably influence people against developing and applying their minds. Or they may be under the false impression that their genetic patterns and upbringing prevent them from increasing the use of their minds.

Suffice it to say that each one of us has the capacity to use the mind in truly magnificent ways, if we are willing to learn the correct modes of applying it — and if we are equally willing to spend whatever time and energy is needed to nurture fully this latent potential. For individuals who already spend much of their time in mental activities, it normally does not require a great amount of additional effort to train the mind to its fullest potential. For those who almost never use their minds, expressing themselves only through their emotions, a significant change in behavior and attitudes is required in order to awaken the sleeping capacities of the mind. But the effort is well worthwhile, for there are few things so pitiful as an unused, unfulfilled mind. It is a condition of paralysis far worse than any crippling disease which restricts its victims to wheelchairs. The paralyzed mind cripples the soul.

The undeveloped mind is like a crystal rock of quartz or ruby. In their natural states, these rocks are often dull and lusterless, and their edges, while perfectly geometrical, are nonetheless rough and uneven. They may glitter and shine to some degree, but until they are cut and polished, they are not very valuable.

Throughout the ages, we have gradually learned more and more about the usefulness of these crystalline stones. At first they were used principally for ornamentation, jewelry, and artwork. Of course, this is still a major use of crystals, but other, more practical uses have been discovered as well. For hundreds of years now, crystals have been ground and polished into lenses for telescopes, microscopes, and cameras. Many phonographic needles are made of diamond crystals, because of their hardness and capacity for conducting electromagnetic energies. Crystals also played an important part in the early development of radios for much the same reason. More recently, crystals have been used as the key element of the most powerful type of laser-producing equipment.

Just so, as we have learned to "cut and polish" the mind, we have come to better appreciate *its* capacities and applications. At first, it was only possible to use the mind for acquiring facts and knowledge, and so the emphasis of instruction was placed on developing the ability to observe those facts and discern, analytically, their value and meaning. But as increasing numbers of humanity acquire these basic skills of thinking, we are discovering that the mind can do much, much more than is commonly supposed. We are learning that the mind can be used to make sense of the often bewildering complexities of life, to solve any problem, to become the focus for creative work, to be a tool for accurate self-comprehension, and to be a great source of stability, convictions, determination, joy, and poise. But most importantly, we are learning that the mind, like the crystal, can be used to focus and intensify light—the light of the soul—thereby harnesssing it productively in the life of the personality.

Indeed, the mind can be justly called the "lens of the soul," for when it is highly polished and correctly focused, it is like a crystal lens which allows us to see without and within. It can be abused, of course, as any lens can—microscopes can be used only to see the dirt under our fingernails and telescopes can be used only to snoop on our neighbors. But these abuses can be avoided by the intelligent person, and in no way detract from the noble purpose for which the mind has been designed.

If we do not develop the mind as fully as we can, our inner eyes remain unfocused—they do not see clearly. As a result, we stumble through our journey of discovery without being able to see quite where we are or understanding how we got there. If, however, we train the mind, we greatly extend our capacity to see, just as putting on eyeglasses can correct the worst conditions of myopia.

Developing the mind and applying it to life is not by any means the only element involved in successfully completing our journey to self-discovery. But it is an indispensable element, for without an active, mature mind, we do not know where to start, nor could we even begin to determine when the journey ends.

MISSTEPS ON OUR WAY

In order to fulfill the noble purposes of the mind, we must learn to observe facts properly and discern their value and meaning; we must develop the ability to evaluate those facts and relate them to our needs, responsibilities, and opportunities; and we must consistently expand our capacity to use knowledge intelligently, skillfully, and productively in our life. To master all three of these aspects of the thinking process requires a profound dedication, the patience to properly train the mind step-by-step, a knowledge of the best way to proceed, and an inspired willingness to experiment.

It also requires a constant vigilance to ensure that we do not fall into harmful habits when using the mind. In developing anything worthwhile, there are always certain errors which must be avoided. A young singer, for example, must take care not to strain his or her vocal chords unduly lest it destroy the quality and tone of the voice. It is for this reason that proper vocal training is so vitally important during the early stages of a singer's development. The same principle is even more applicable in training the mind, because pitfalls and risks seem to lurk at every stage of growth.

Once we develop bad habits in using the mind, they are hard to break, just as bad habits in using language skills for speaking, writing, or listening are not easily overcome. Even literate people who fall into the bad practice of mispronouncing or misspelling certain words find it difficult to correct the errors, because they do not recognize the mistake. Just so, if we fall into the bad mental habit of periodically turning off the mind—for example, through the practice of a misguided form of meditation—it could be a hard pattern of behavior to shake. First of all, we would probably be blind to the undesirability of this habit; indeed, we might well believe it worthwhile to empty the mind frequently and stop thinking. We would perhaps contend that such a practice "refreshes" the mind. Of course, nothing is farther from the truth; such practices encourage *mindlessness,* but we would not see this. Secondly, when we finally did awaken to the fact that our bad habit had numbed the mind, it would require constant retraining over a period of time to return to a healthy state of thinking.

These bad mental habits can be considered "missteps" on our journey to self-discovery and enlightenment—faults which delay the progress we ought to be making. They cost us valuable time and cause a measure of suffering, but they can be corrected. Indeed, there is no reason why we cannot learn to avoid making the misstep in the first place! Children who are taught correct pronunciation and spelling at an early age, for example, and are simultaneously taught to *respect* literacy, have no difficulty speaking and writing lucidly as adults. But people who are not properly trained as children find it immensely more difficult to learn the same elementary skills in their later years. It is no different in training the mind; the neophyte who learns what to avoid and what to stress will have a great advantage over the fellow who seeks enlightenment haphazardly. And the person who nurtures a deep sense of appreciation for the proper uses of the mind will likewise progress more rapidly than the individual who does not.

Just as there are innumerable mistakes which can be made in the use of language skills, there are likewise many possible missteps to be anticipated by the intelligent individual seeking to train his mind. In order to fully appreciate the proper steps involved in developing the mind, it is wise to begin by analyzing the more common and dangerous missteps, to understand why they are improper and how they can be corrected.

Some of these missteps, for example, are caused by being too passive when using the mind. These misuses include:

Illogical thinking. The mind has been designed to operate logically, by placing thoughts in their proper order and drawing appropriate conclusions from the patterns which emerge as a result. Beginning thinkers, however, often fall into the disconcerting habit of dumping all their thoughts into a common pile, without bothering to sort them out. Their conclusions are therefore illogical and rather useless. Such careless, passive thinkers confuse priorities, make unwarranted assumptions, and become hopelessly entangled in irrelevancies. Illogical thought is very much like unstructured speech — an incoherent "word salad" in which all the ingredients have been tossed to the point of being incomprehensible. Obviously, the cure for illogical thinking is the study of logic and its application. Mathematics, with its emphasis on rigorous proofs, can be an excellent stimulus of logical thinking.

Intellectual voyeurism. Some people use their minds just to collect facts and ideas, without processing them or using them productively. At its best, this is an extremely passive use of the mind and cannot be considered genuine thinking. At its worst, it is an invasion of the mental privacy of others: snooping for gossip and scavenging for stealable ideas. Intellectual voyeurs operate on the assumption that by associating with grand thoughts and ideas, they will learn to think. Useful thought, however, cannot be acquired by osmosis; only when we *build* facts into valid structures of thought do we begin to fulfill the design of the mind. Intellectual voyeurism is like reciting a Shakespearean sonnet and then believing that we are a poet, too — or worse, claiming to be the author. To correct this problem, we must start using the mind more actively. Instead of annexing the ideas of other people, we must make our own observations, form our own conclusions, and put our own ideas to work.

Haphazard perception. In using the mind to observe life, we must take care to perceive not just the literal appearance of objects, ideas, and happenings, but also the subtle shades of meaning and purpose. Especially when the mind has not been developed very much, it is possible to miss most of the relevant observations connected with any idea. This in turn leads to false assumptions and inaccurate conclusions. It is something like trying to listen to a university professor discourse on Aristotelian logic when all we can understand is pidgin English or ghetto slang. Haphazard perception is a common failing of fundamentalists who insist on interpreting the Bible literally, thereby misunderstanding its spiritual truths. They are too lazy to place the ideas they read in their fullest, symbolic contexts. The cure for haphazard perception lies in increasing our ability to see implications, assumptions, parallels, and the subtleties of thought.

Shallow-mindedness. Even when perception is accurate, the thinking process can be upset by superficial cognition—thinking about a problem just long enough to get a tiny clue to the answer, then mistaking that first clue for the whole solution. The shallow-minded person becomes drunk on insubstantial inspiration and must learn the virtue of being thorough in his thinking. As Alexander Pope put it:

> A little learning is a dang'rous thing;
> Drink deep, or taste not the Pierian spring:
> There shallow draughts intoxicate the brain,
> And drinking largely sobers us again.

This particular misstep is especially common among people developing the intuitive faculties of the mind. By being shallow-minded we are like the cub reporter who learns that too many adjectives can slow down a news story—and so never uses any.

Mental conformity. In its fullest sense, thinking includes the processing of observations we make, by evaluating them and applying them to life. Some of us, however, try to take short cuts by filtering our thoughts through set formulae, dogma, or stereotyped beliefs. This is the equivalent of being a television script writer who always uses the same plot for all of his shows, just changing names, dates, and locations. Taking these short cuts sabotages the thinking process, because it eliminates the step of evaluating our observations. This problem is corrected by considering each idea on its merits, not by set formula.

Heedlessness. As we develop the mind and contact our higher intelligence, we begin to receive ideas, plans, warnings, and guidance. Some of this inspiration comes through inner whispers, some through the good advice of friends. The wise person pays heed to this help and puts it to work in his life, but many of us ignore it. We have not fully learned that we are responsible for our lives and must act constructively with the opportunities and help which comes to us. We are still too passive, perhaps believing that just being nice is enough to complete our journey, perhaps believing in the false notion of fatalism—that our lives are hopelessly beyond our control and therefore not affected by what we do. By being heedless, we become like a hermit who reads nothing, listens to no radio or television, and refuses to talk to anyone.

Being too theoretical. By training the mind, we gain the capacity to soar to great heights and begin thinking in purely abstract ways. Some people who start working at these higher levels, however, forget that the mind is designed to be a very practical instrument for solving problems, for creating better life conditions, for improving relationships, and for helping us on our journey of discovery. They do not bother to translate the great abstract truths into ideas which are understandable to others and projects helpful to humanity. They become too theoretical. In this way, they are like spiritual leaders who speak only in generalities, platitudes, and nonsensical "koans"; when asked to say something useful, they reply it is impossible to express great truths in words. This excuse is one of the great fallacies of our age; what makes any truth true is the fact that it *can be* manifested physically, it *can be* described in spoken and written words, and it *can be* applied to our everyday life. People who tend to be too theoretical need to roll up their sleeves and start putting their theories to work for the benefit of mankind.

Passiveness, of course, is not the only cause of mental missteps. Problems also arise if we try developing the mind without understanding the basic ideals it is designed to serve. Without an appreciation of these ideals, it is possible to fall into the following bad mental habits:

Sophistry, the pursuit of false or insignificant knowledge. To many of us, life appears to be no more meaningful than a game—and the mind, a device for playing it. If we accept this notion as a basic assumption, then obviously we care little whether we deal with accurate or false information. Indeed, there may be occasions when blatantly false doctrines and facts will seem to serve our "game plan" more conveniently than the truth. Or, we use the mind merely to entertain ourself and others with trivia, gossip, and ephemeral facts. Indulging in sophistry is something like a politician responding to pointed questions with double talk designed to cover up the true answers and mislead the public—or like a reporter attending a Presidential press conference and then reporting only what the President was wearing, not what he talked about. Sophistry is a very dangerous pitfall, because the person who practices it quickly deceives himself as well as everyone else. The cure for it is to realize that life does have meaning and we are responsible for what we do, what we say, and how we use our talents and opportunities. The mind is not a plaything; it is designed to be used nobly. Therefore, we must increase our resolve to behave nobly, to act with integrity, and to respect the divine roots of knowledge and wisdom by applying them to life!

Rationalization. The mind has been designed to be the supervisor of the emotions and body, but some people turn it into a servant which defends the cravings and fears of the lower personality. Far from being harnessed to discipline these selfish elements, the mind is used to invent alibis and excuses to "justify" them. Such misuse of the mind turns our inner life topsy-turvy; instead of discerning the noble values of life, the mind ends up rationalizing away the most petty tendencies within us. In this way, it becomes like a child who has not yet developed many language skills and uses his voice primarily to cry and fuss, whenever his bodily cravings and desires are not satisfied. The only way to modify this bad mental habit is to grow up and begin using the mind more maturely, for expressing inner ideals and convictions.

Concretism. Some people are so hypnotized by their physical senses that they reject the reality of anything they cannot concretely see or touch. They believe emotions and thoughts exist only in the physical brain; they scoff at faith, intuition, and human ideals as signs of superstition. In the process, they deny the existence of all meaning and purpose, reducing life to a purely mechanical level. This attitude is like believing that English is the only language on earth, because all the newspapers and books in this country are printed in it. Concretism makes it very hard to develop the mind adequately, because it rejects its basic principles and design. This misstep is overcome by learning that the mind's greatest function is to link the inner ideals of the soul with the outer forms of life.

Other mental missteps stem from being too small-minded in the way we approach life. Motivated by selfishness, bigotry, and vainglory, our mind builds boxes which entrap us and greatly limit our perspectives. These abuses of the thinking apparatus include:

Narrow-mindedness. In order to develop the analytical function of the mind, it is necessary to dissect facts, see how they differ from each other, and separate them into appropriate groupings. If we forget that analysis is just one function of a complete mind, however, it is easy to become extremely narrow in our outlook, seeing only the trees and forgetting that they compose a forest. It is possible to focus so much attention on little details that we become entirely absorbed in them; as a result, our thoughts and conclusions become trivialized. This is a self-imposed limitation, much like insisting on using only verbs beginning with the letter "t" in our conversations. The antidote for narrow-mindedness is remembering that analysis must always be followed by synthesis, thus reintegrating the dissected facts into a larger, more inclusive overview.

Mental miserliness. Selfish people dislike sharing

their possessions and using them to help others, and this trait can extend into the realm of the mind as well. Such people use their minds merely to hoard as many good ideas as they can; instead of applying them and doing something useful with them, they keep them to themselves. These Fagins of facts become very secretive, saying as little about their thoughts as possible, lest someone steal them. Miserliness can be compared to the person who jots down all of his ideas in a secret code only he understands, so only he will be able to use them. This trait is overcome by realizing there is such an abundance of good ideas within the mind of God that we can freely put them to work for the benefit of everyone — and still have other ideas available for future use!

Arrogance. As we develop legitimate skills in the use of the mind and the art of living, we grow confident in our ability to apply these skills effectively. But some people become falsely confident in their abilities when they really have not done much to develop them; they become convinced that their opinions are correct and what they do is inspired. Such false confidence and unsubstantiated superiority is arrogance, a problem the traditional bigot commonly falls into. The arrogant person can be compared to the self-professed expert who always speaks and writes in the exclamatory mood — but who has only learned the present tense! In his effort to impress everyone with his superiority, he loudly proclaims his obvious deficiencies for all to see. The best way for such a person to correct his error is to practice humility — to make an objective analysis of just what he does know and not pretend to anything greater than that.

Doubting. An important part of training the mind is learning not to willy-nilly believe everything we hear, read, or observe. We must learn to be objective, and so intelligent doubting—the ability to put an idea we do not fully understand "on the shelf" for further consideration, until we can prove or disprove its correctness—is a valuable skill to develop. But too often we overemphasize our doubts, by distrusting our abilities, by questioning the competence or good intentions of our friends, or by disbelieving in the presence of intelligence in the universe. This mental misstep is somewhat akin to being afraid to say anything, lest we choose the wrong words and suffer embarrassment. Unintelligent doubting interferes with our efforts to build a stable outlook on life, as it introduces unnecessary uncertainty. The history of science is filled with examples of men and women with small minds doubting the discoveries and theories of brilliant innovators—even after the discoveries had been proven! Even today, many people make fools of themselves, by doubting the validity of psychic phenomena, life after death, and the existence of the soul, although all of these have been demonstrated to be real hundreds of times over—and by such eminent scientists as Sir Oliver Lodge and Sir William Crookes. Unintelligent doubting is often just an excuse for mental laziness, a disguise for bigotry, and a coverup for the fear of different viewpoints. It is corrected by becoming more appreciative of the spirit of discovery—and by eliminating any tendencies to be afraid of finding out what life signifies.

Not all misuses of the mind harm only the person trying to make progress on his journey to self-discovery. When the mind is used maliciously, as a weapon, it can hurt other people and civilization as well. Great danger comes from using the mind in these ways, because we *are* accountable for our actions, thoughts, and deeds. The bad mental habits founded in malice include:

Cynicism. Unchecked, a tendency to doubt can quickly fester into the disease of cynicism, in which we scoff at all ideas, theories, and human qualities because we cannot be one hundred percent certain they are flawless. Like the hunchback who condemns the sun for having sunspots and occasional eclipses, the cynic sees only imperfection and therefore rejects all of life. He is like a grammarian who refuses to correspond with his mother, because she misspells words in her letters. Cynicism is a mental cancer that rapidly kills the mind, because it makes its victim unable to discern the noble values of life—which is one of the primary purposes of the mind. To recover, the cynic must begin to realize that in any process of evolution, imperfection may for long periods of time be more prominent than perfection. But because life is evolving, the ultimate attainment of perfection is guaranteed. Therefore, the cynic must cultivate hope and work to build civilization, not undermine it.

Intellectual nihilism and anarchism. Many people have such a fascination with chaos or fear of order that they consistently ignore the fact that the mind is designed to find and impose structure. Rejecting any kind of discipline or principle, they believe there are no real ideas or facts, just opinions and beliefs. They claim everything is relative and try to prove it by being as intellectually confusing as possible. The worst of the lot become mental bomb-throwers and assassins of rational concepts, senselessly attacking any pattern of order which comes to their attention. Mental anarchy is well satirized by comics who deliberately use malapropisms in their speech, or spew forth rapid-fire and utterly garbled phrases that destroy all meaning and sense. The lives of intellectual nihilists and anarchists reflect the disorder of their minds. This misstep can only be corrected by recognizing that all of life is based on patterns and principles; the mind, therefore, must be used to discern the order inherent in our responsibilities, our opportunities, and the events of life.

Criticism. As we develop our ability to make correct observations, it becomes easier to see the failings, weaknesses, and mistakes of others. However, using the mind to find fault and harshly condemn the shortcomings of others is not a practice which fulfills the noble purposes of the mind. Criticism is immature and corrosive. It is like being a gossip who is interested in discerning truth only when it is bad enough that he does not have to lie in order to hurt or titillate others. Correcting this trait is mostly a question of learning balance and compassion. Certainly there is no value in pretending that other people do not have flaws or shortcomings; the balanced approach is to demonstrate within our own life that failings can be overcome — and it is important to do so. This approach does far more good than simply condemning the wrongness in others.

Defensiveness or intellectual paranoia. This problem is much the same as criticism, only intensified. The mind is used to keep others away from us, lest their ideas hurt us. Usually what we are trying to defend is hardly worth the trouble — a closed mind built of illogical prejudices and misconceptions. Defensiveness, therefore, is often just a means of enhancing our own ego by default. It is something like a person who writes threatening letters to others so they will believe he has something worth protecting. It is cured by realizing that the only mental treasures worth defending are the qualities of consciousness we already share with all other people, at inner levels, and therefore need no protection. Moreover, instead of constantly emphasizing the deficiencies of others and the ways in which they differ from us, we must make a point of noticing their strengths and good qualities, and how they are similar to us.

Mental bullying. Because the mind is used in creativity, it has the capacity to dynamically project ideas into manifestation. When a person with strong convictions, a rigid mind, and a fanatical will deals with other people, he often misuses this projective capacity to dominate, intimidate, manipulate, and influence them, almost like a tinhorn dictator imposing his wishes on the public. Not uncommonly, this bullying occurs telepathically, with the victims unaware of what is happening. In extreme cases, it becomes a form of brainwashing; the free will of other people is violated and they are used to execute the selfish purposes of the bully. Unfortunately, some of the more popular self-improvement courses of today feature precisely this kind of mental bullying; the minds of students are brazenly enslaved for the purpose of proselytizing others. Rather than building the mind, the mental bully controls it, imprisons it, and all but wipes it out. To overcome this pitfall, the bully must realize that instead of creating thoughtforms which ensnare others, it is preferable to create thoughtforms that will inspire, help, and heal others. This is the creative use of the projective capacity and will allow him to grow, not stagnate. As for the victim of mental bullying, he must learn to discriminate between legitimate friends, teachers, and associates on the one hand and "wolves in sheep's clothing" on the other. Secondly, the victim must strengthen his own mind so that it can resist the intrusion of bullies, by cultivating courage, an appreciation of ideals, and right understanding.

In addition, a number of mental missteps are caused by our silliness and childlike attitudes toward personal growth. The person who succumbs to these dangers does not understand the great power and purpose of the mind and continues to believe that good intentions are the only things which count in life. As a consequence, he develops some or all of the following problems:

Astralism masquerading as thinking. At times our attempts at thinking clearly about life are overwhelmed by sentimentality, fantasy, and the collective wish life of the human race. Instead of courageously facing a difficult situation at home or work, for example, we simply pretend nothing is wrong. Such fantasies destroy our mental integrity and objectivity. We become like a person who speaks entirely by quoting lines from television commercials or musical comedies, filling his head with the most banal junk. Astralism is corrected by increasing our love for truth.

Spiritual stupidity. Not understanding the role and purpose of the mind, some people seeking spiritual attainment try to bypass the mind and tune in directly to "pure blissful wisdom." They make no effort to train the mind, developing only a contempt for intellectual effort, logical thinking, and creative activity. As a result, they end up with a zero mentality; if they do succeed in contacting pure wisdom, which is possible, they nevertheless cannot comprehend it or put it to work. They fail to recognize that the mind is the vehicle for translating pure wisdom into practical knowledge. Thus, they become transcendent idiots, enlightened fools. Their behavior can be compared to the antics of the charismatics who fall into trances and begin babbling, but are unable to translate what they say or comprehend its meaning. The cure for th s bad habit is to see that the mind does have a divine purpose which must not be ignored if we are to fulf ll our destiny; we must train it to operate in mundane as well as in spiritual ways.

Mental mushiness, the sanctification of mere niceness. The spiritually stupid person often develops another bad mental habit as well: out of fear of *appearing* critical or bigoted, he suspends his ability to evaluate conditions, form convictions, and act upon them. He becomes simply a "mellow fellow," totally undiscerning, bland, and vapid. He *seems* to exhibit spirituality, in that he is able to tolerate almost all and everything, but it is the type of "spirituality" which would have disapproved — gently, of course — of Jesus's condemnation of the Pharisees and Sadducees or His eviction of the money-changers from the temple. Because he has stopped thinking, the mental mushhead cannot see that there is a difference between good and evil, between what is constructive and what is useless, and between reality and wishes. The mushhead is like the person who speaks quietly, sweetly, and inoffensively, but always in a monotone, no matter what he is talking about. The nouns and verbs tumble out of his mouth, but have no character or significance. Far from being a necessary attribute of spirituality, as some insist, mental mushiness is a detriment to self-discovery. To overcome it, we must recognize our responsibilities to the advancement of human civilization and the fulfillment of God's Plan, and train the mind to participate actively in this work.

Eccentricity. Thinking is a powerful process, far more powerful than many people suspect. As we begin working in the realm of ideas, we contact forces and energies of far greater potency than the average person deals with. If we do not properly train our personality system to use these energies productively, they will generally manifest in counter-productive ways: by making our bad habits worse, by obsessing us with fanatical drives and goals, and by producing various eccentricities which become "false centers" of our focus and work. History is filled with examples of budding mental giants who poured valuable time and energy into perfectly worthless pursuits, simply because they had not learned to control the magnificent potency of grand ideas. This problem is akin to the lecturer who becomes so transported by his rhetoric and flowery phrases that he forgets the reason why he is on the dais, speaking. It is conquered in two ways: by disciplining our emotions and body while training the mind, so that our bad habits will not be aggravated by the greater power we contact; and by putting our creative ideas to work as quickly and as fully as possible, thereby safely "grounding" the dynamic mental energy associated with them.

None of these bad mental habits, these missteps on our journey of self-discovery, will completely block our progress. But any one of them can seriously delay our efforts and cause us to wander about in confusion, like brave Odysseus, until we learn to overcome it and proceed correctly. Only then can the unfoldment of the mind in its glory occur.

MANUFACTURING WISDOM

The success of any venture depends largely on the goals established in the beginning. If, in pursuing the development of the mind, we strive merely for the ability to work with facts and knowledge, we will achieve different results than if our goal is to master the expression of wisdom in our life. Knowledge has its usefulness, but simply gathering and winnowing knowledge does not fulfill the purpose of the mind, which is to be the lens of the soul, a crystal through which wisdom can be directed. As the French mathematician Henri Poincaré put it, "Science is built up with facts, as a house is with stones. But a collection of facts is no more a science than a heap of stones is a house." In other words, the true use of the mind deals with wisdom, not knowledge, just as the true nature of a house lies in its purpose and use, not its structure.

Knowledge can be picked up as easily as picking up stones, but the acquisition of wisdom is a bit more complex. Wisdom does not exist in tangible forms, ready to be added to our waiting mind. The principles of wisdom do exist, intangibly, but for us to acquire wisdom personally, we must *create it* within our own consciousness, by distilling facts and knowledge to their most sublime essence. It is not possible merely to touch wisdom, Midas-like, and be transformed into a wise person. It must be manufactured, and it can only be manufactured by a mature, properly trained mind. The functional steps in creating wisdom are fivefold:

First, the mind must be trained in the art of skillful observation. If we make mistakes in observing life, our objectivity — a necessary ingredient in wisdom — will be prejudiced from the very beginning. There is truly an enormous amount of observable data, phenomena, ideas, and knowledge all about us, waiting to be discovered by our keen and watchful eye. Sadly, many scientists and budding thinkers do not understand this simple fact. Instead of looking about themselves objectively to find out what life is like, they begin with a pet theory and then look only for phenomena which substantiate their beliefs. This approach does not honor the basic spirit of discovery or do justice to the knowledge and understanding potentially available to us. To take advantage of knowledge, we must actively seek it — by reading, talking with informed people, circulating through society and the world, and always being alert for significance. In addition, we must train ourself to look for the subtle shades of meaning which relate the physical forms to nonphysical phenomena — the psychic levels of awareness. Otherwise, we will be dealing with such a tiny fragment of life that it will be impossible to create wisdom. Above all, we must learn to observe *everything* of importance. Many of us are very careless in our observations; we miss most of what is happening in life. This first step in creating wisdom is much like a manufacturing firm sending its agents throughout the world searching for raw materials, always looking for new sources of better quality.

Next, the observed data must be analyzed in the "laboratories" of the mind, through the twin processes of discrimination and discernment. Discrimination is a test for determining which observations are useful and pertinent to our needs, and which are irrelevant. It is a capacity many people have yet to develop to any significant degree, which explains why we get caught up in purposeless activities so frequently. Discrimination's brother, discernment, is the ability to assay the relative value of data which has passed the test of discrimination. It sees how much any piece of accepted data reflects or expresses the principles of wisdom — the ideals of human evolution and the purposes of divine mind. This second step in creating wisdom can be compared to the testing of raw materials by a company's quality control unit.

Then, the analyzed data must be integrated or assimilated into our general body of knowledge and understanding, by reviewing it and comparing it with previous knowledge, standards, memories, and principles. Only a mind with a well-developed capacity for thinking logically and orderly will be able to integrate new data effectively, because so much depends on being able to see how information and ideas fit in with each other. We integrate false data by remembering what is true; for example, if someone claims the earth is flat, we integrate his statement by recalling the proof that the world is spherical. We integrate true data by revising older ideas in the light of our new input, altering our interpretation of memories as needed, and weighing the implications of the new information. This step of integration is equivalent to the manufacturing activity of combining together various raw materials for the purpose of creating useful alloys.

Fourth, the new information or conclusions we have integrated into our consciousness must be applied to our daily activities and used in guiding our conduct. We formulate new plans on the basis of our greater understanding, reorder our priorities, embark on new lines of creative expression, revise our attitudes and convictions, and construe new responsibilities and duties. Of course, it is not just enough to think about these changes abstractly; we must also honor and respect them by faithfully acting in accordance with them. This step corresponds to the actual manufacture of the finished product from the alloys and raw materials.

The creation of wisdom is completed by realizing the full significance and purpose of the ideas we have been dealing with. Realization can occur in one of two ways. The first builds gradually: by putting our ideas to work successfully in daily life over a long period of time, always studying their consequences and benefits, we eventually absorb into our awareness an intuitive sense of their full meaning and value. The second is a more advanced stage: by focusing our intuition directly on the abstract essence of these ideas, we may be able to achieve a mystical identification with this essence and thereby distill the same comprehension instantly. In either case, this final stage is similar to selling the manufactured product to those who need it and receiving compensation for it; realization is the profit of our mental labors, which can be reinvested in future growth.

It should be clear from this analogy that the manufacture of wisdom is always a thoroughly active process, in which the mind is used in practical ways: to solve problems of work and home, to fulfill commitments, to enrich the quality of our self-expression, and to develop new opportunities for growth. Purposeful activity is the very heart of training the mind. Indeed, the education of the human mind can be neatly reduced to three succinct "training rules":

1. The mind is developed by using it in the *activity* of seeking to comprehend our relationship to our higher self.

2. The mind is developed by using it in the *activity* of seeking to comprehend our relationship to the world around us.

3. The mind is developed by using it in the *activity* of seeking to comprehend our relationship with humanity as a whole.

As long as this basic theme of using the mind actively is maintained and honored, the mind will unfold according to its fundamental design. Within this context, then, a number of more specific suggestions for training the mind can be given, one for each of the five steps in the process of manufacturing wisdom.

We must focus our mind and intelligence on the life about us, making careful and full observations. If necessary, this effort can be assisted by keeping a daily journal in which we list the interesting and important observations made during the course of our activities. But the process of observing must become a constant interest, not just something which produces grist for a diary. To train the mind, we must be constantly alert, noticing as much as we can — never slumping off into boredom or half-attention.

We must read widely in the works of intelligent authors, making an effort to comprehend their ideas. This activity sharpens our analytical capacity, expands the scope of our knowledge, and stimulates the mind. Often in reading we actually begin communing with the thoughtforms created by the author while writing the book. Of course, part of learning discrimination and discernment comes from choosing the right books to read. As a general rule, most dime-store novels and semifiction posing as nonfiction will not help us train the mind. Neither will books which ask us to believe their contents, rather than think about them. But excellent fiction (including science fiction), the works of profound thinkers, and books on man, his civilization, scientific knowledge, and environment are of immense value.

We must discuss ideas and important topics with friends who are knowledgeable on those subjects. In this way, we obtain different perspectives, fresh ideas, and new information, which help clarify our thinking. Of course, if we only discuss ideas with people with untrained minds, we are likely to perpetuate prejudices and mistaken opinions. Therefore, it is also important to seek out experts and "pick their brains." The chance to do this is one of the great opportunities afforded by a college education; it is also one of the unheralded fringe benefits of working in certain large corporations. Great value can also be gained by holding frequent conversations with our own soul—the inner oracle. As much as possible, we must train ourself to approach ideas, projects, and information from the perspective of this inner oracle. Such insight is obtained by considering the deepest meanings and purposes of the data under scrutiny.

We must learn to contemplate the fullness of ideas. In its purest meaning, contemplation is the mental process of formulating specific ways to apply abstract ideas and ideals, for the benefit of humanity. In contemplation, we project ideas, study their probable consequences, try to anticipate difficulties, and visualize the end results of our mental activity. We deal with implications and applications. The ability to contemplate can be acquired most rapidly through a daily practice of a proper form of meditation.

We must cautiously experiment with ideas, always trying to discover the best way of applying them. The heart of this experimentation lies in asking ourself many speculative questions. How can we use this knowledge? What is the significance of that set of events? If we change our behavior in this aspect of life, how will other people react? If a certain assumption is true, how does it change the conclusions we have already made? In fact, in training the mind it is important never to stop asking these questions nor end our experiments in living.

By practicing these techniques, we polish the lens of the mind, so it becomes more capable of focusing the brilliant light of the soul. But it is important to choose the right subjects for our practice. If we direct the power of the mind only to theoretical speculation, we may soon find ourself more confused then ever. If we engage it in excessive criticism and pessimism, we may quickly lose control of the power we have harnessed.

The best subjects, always, would be ourself and our involvement in the rest of life. We should use the mind, for example, to determine our personal purpose in life, as well as the principles and ethics by which we express ourself and treat others. The mind is uniquely suited for this activity, as its five-dimensional nature lets every conviction we form become a central core of stability producing great strength of character. Then, too, we should exercise the mind by searching for the order of life and society, and discovering how we can better cooperate with it. We should examine the invisible laws which govern right human relationships, the factors which lead to the flowering of opportunities, and the dynamic forces controlling the cyclic sequence of events. The mind can discern these intangible patterns and the order of life, because its very nature is rooted in divine order. And it can show us how to better cooperate with them and generate a more refined level of order, by developing intelligent plans, establishing greater consistency in the way we respond to opportunities and challenges, acting with fairness and integrity, and cultivating efficiency and effectiveness in all we do.

One of the most practical ways to focus the power of the mind is to define the meaning and purpose of the activities of life: the meaning and purpose of the job we hold; the meaning and purpose of our marriage, of being a parent, and of having friendships; the meaning and purpose of being a citizen; the meaning and purpose of various conditions of life; and the meaning and purpose of being human. If we take the time to define these values in their fullest implications, we will acquire tremendous new insight, an inpouring of creative ideas, and a greater awareness *that this business of living is indeed useful and productive!*

Similarly, we should use the mind to review the commitments we have made to ourself, to others, and to life; to accept our responsibilities and duties; and to formulate plans for better fulfilling them. As we do, we will gradually understand that opportunities are not created by wishing for them; they are created by becoming competent and by using our competence for the benefit of mankind. We will also learn that the mind can be usefully applied in rendering service and help to others, to society, and to the institutions of humanity. The role of the mind in this work is to discern the true needs of others, the divine ideals to be honored in filling those needs, and the most effective way of doing the work.

As our interest in serving divine purpose evolves, we should also apply the mind to discerning the hidden love and perfection behind all living phenomena, looking for the divine seeds or archetypal forces which animate life. By asking ourself, through contemplation, what purposes are being served by events and conditions, we gradually achieve a level of revelation most people do not even believe possible. We also find that the mind can be used to discern the symbolic within the real and to recognize how each element of life fits into the wholeness of life. As a result, we develop the ability to see the forest within the leaf, beauty within the petal of a flower, joy in the song of a bird, and the Christ within the human being.

As this understanding of the wholeness of life develops, it likewise becomes possible to use the mind skillfully to solve problems and make intelligent decisions. The mind can become quite expert in analyzing conditions, seeing what we lack, and then leading the effort to cultivate it. Indeed, this is a very useful model for solving problems and making decisions. But it must be applied logically and objectively. Too many people deepen their difficulties by defining their problems superstitiously, in terms of what they are afraid might happen, or what they assume others are doing to them, or how they are being victimized. They refuse to consider what they are contributing to their problems. Such attitudes continually sabotage our better efforts to cultivate the mind and enrich the art of living. They are signs of weakness in understanding. It requires great courage to penetrate our prejudices, self-deceptions, and illusions—but courage is one of the virtues of the noble human mind, the mind which has been trained to solve problems and make intelligent decisions.

Possibly the best subject for training the mind, though, is creative activity, not only in the arts and sciences but even more importantly in our handling of responsibility, friendship, and opportunity. The mind links us to those deeper levels of being at which inspiration and guidance reside. It lets us seize brilliant ideas and shape them into plans, ideals, new attitudes, and qualities of self-expression which transform the work we do and our personal behavior. As we pursue creative work, we exercise the mind to its fullest, for no activity of human living demands so much—or brings greater rewards.

Always, it is important to understand that nothing stimulates the development of the mind more effectively than the constant activity of applying it and using it in the daily challenges of living—the work we do the relationships we forge, the service we perform, and the opportunities we invoke. The mind does not develop if we sit around, idly daydreaming; conceived in activity, it must be nurtured in activity!

Nevertheless, if this concept is fully understood and accepted, it can also be beneficial to recognize that the mind can be stimulated from within as well as without. The mind has its roots in our inner life, after all, and operates best when harnessed by the light and wisdom of the soul. The training of the mind, therefore, can be powerfully assisted by the intelligent practice of correct forms of meditation. The use of meditative techniques should never supplant the methods of developing the mind already described, but complement them.

In its purest form, meditation is a practice which links the mind with the soul, for the purpose of bringing heaven to earth — to solve problems, act creatively, achieve greater understanding of the meanings and purposes of life, and enrich the quality of the human experience. Meditation should always be a very active process, in which the mind is exercised, stretched, and attuned to the soul. It should *never* become passive. Unfortunately, this is an area of great confusion today, for many people do practice passive meditative techniques, in which they empty their minds and think militantly upon absolutely nothing at all. Such practices numb the intelligence and are gravely dangerous to our mental well-being. They harm the development and competence of the mind, rather than assist it.

One other distortion of meditation deserves mention, too, as it can also interfere with the training of the mind — the belief that the practice of meditation is a guarantee of spirituality. Like any mental technique, meditation is only a means to an end. If practiced wisely, it can do much to strengthen our mental skills and help us contact divine levels of consciousness. It can accelerate our efforts to converse with the higher self and learn the true nature of contemplation, as well as to help us break through the limitations of our concrete thoughts and enter into the abstract world of archetypes and ideals. But meditation is useful only when combined with ever-increasing involvement and responsibility in daily life. It should never become an escape from problems nor a withdrawal from life. The true power of meditation leads us into greater competence, knowledge, and wisdom.

Indeed, it is wisdom that we seek: not some facile "wisdom" which accepts everything and understands nothing, but practical wisdom we have manufactured in the foundries and refineries of our life. Wisdom that leads us to self-discovery. Wisdom which enables us to be a meaningful part of human civilization. Most of all, wisdom that reveals to us the face of God.

THE FULL LIGHT OF DAY

Before embarking on our journey of discovering the mind, it would be helpful to have a means for evaluating whether or not we are making progress. Many people frustrate themselves by judging their efforts by the final goal they hope to achieve and failing to give themselves credit for the important but smaller steps made along the way. Our success in living, however, is not measured by reaching the ultimate goal — it is measured by the step-by-step progress made in heading for the goal. Success is measured by our minor triumphs at work, at home, and in the community.

Fortunately, there are many such minor triumphs on

the journey of self-discovery, and they deserve to be given proper credit. Whenever we act with greater detachment, dispassion, and objectivity in handling facts, plans, and decisions, the mind has grown stronger. It has learned to set aside, at least in part, its prejudices, feelings, and fears and analyze life with new logic and clarity. Of course, if all we have done is retreat into a state of emotional blandness and niceness, that would not amount to much of an accomplishment. But the ability to relate ideas in a meaningful way to our needs, responsibilites, opportunities, and creativity is a triumph — and should be recognized.

Similarly, whenever we achieve greater consistency in thinking and self-expression, it is a sign that we have mastered the orderliness of thought. The recognition that we have succeeded may come at a moment of temptation when we find we *do* have the strength not to succumb, or as the result of discovering we are more firmly rooted in principles, ideals, and ethical standards than before.

Another clear sign of progress is the ability to perceive elements of life we have previously ignored. Anytime we become aware of subtle shades of meaning or understand hidden implications, our mental capacities have grown. Whenever we are able to pierce the bias, propaganda, or lying of con artists and tricksters, our abilities to discern life have increased. Often, this recognition comes as a result of understanding aspects of life which had earlier puzzled us. Perhaps we see that certain conditions of life just are not as important as we once believed them to be, and are now willing to let go of them. That is evidence of success! So is the ability to recognize blind spots, understand the meaning of past events, and better appreciate our talents.

Above all, whenever we live more gracefully, wisely, and compassionately, it is a sign of growth. As we train the mind, we are able to *do* more and *be* more in life. Therefore, every time we muster new dignity, courage, and patience in the face of adversity, it is an indication that we have become more mature. Every time we perform our duties with a bit more efficiency and skill, it is a sign that we have harnessed more of the power of the mind and learned to apply it.

Eventually, through years of hard work, we string together a succession of these small but important triumphs, and thereby create a *mature mind* — a mind which understands its purpose and is able to express itself with poise and dignity. Like a Churchill, Lincoln, or Shakespeare, who is able to express ideas and human truths in moving, witty, and trenchant words, the mature mind is capable of capturing the essence of human experience and sharing it in deed and gesture with others.

As we achieve this maturity of the mind, we become poised, filled with the light of the soul. We can never be shaken, no matter what may happen. This is not to imply that we are rigid; we are perfectly capable of adapting to changes which occur. But through the development of the mind, we have discovered the deepest elements of humanity within us, and we are poised in their strength.

We likewise acquire a greater sense of responsibility, recognizing more fully the consequences of our actions and their implications. As a result, we become orderly and logical in all that we do. We think and act with a measure of consistency which is both reliable and responsive to the guidance of the soul. Having discovered a larger measure of our inward parts, we no longer behave whimsically. We act with wisdom, instead of reacting to life blindly and fearfully.

By cultivating a mature mind, we demonstrate to ourself our competence in managing the affairs of life; we know that we are no longer dependent upon the vagaries of fortune or luck. Having found peace within, we are able to carry the peace within us into the midst of great activity in the outer world, thereby achieving our goals.

A mature mind enables us to work at abstract levels as comfortably as the levels of form. We are able to integrate the intangible with the tangible, giving life to creative ideas, new ethics, and greater compassion. Moreover, we are able to act on these multiple levels of mind without confusion, knowing our role and place in life and working steadfastly to honor them. As a result, we find joy and fulfillment—even in bringing to fruition the smallest aspect of our life or work. We know we are involved in meaningful activity and comprehend why it is significant, letting us justifiably take pride in all we accomplish.

But the mature mind represents far more than even all of this. It is the crystal lens through which the light of the soul shines, the prism through which divine will flows and then separates into its constituent expressions of dignity, nobility, self-determination, courage, sacrifice, strength, and unity. From the mature and focused crystal of the mind, these qualities of spirit will radiate forth into the life and world around us, inspiring everyone we contact, quickening their maturity, and leading the way for those who choose to follow. At times, this light is so intense that even our mature mind believes the crystal will surely shatter, but it does not. It adds new facets, new dimensions, and new potency.

The power and light of the soul can shine only

through a mind which has been properly trained and developed. If the mind were unable to focus and radiate the light intelligently, stimulating it in this way might well cause it to become destructive. It is immensely important to appreciate the integrity and maturity required to handle these quantities of power—and to know that the service of God requires not just faith and hope, but also an enlightened mind. Through faith and hope, we initiate our spiritual journey, but it is the light of the mind which illumines the path we must tread. Faith gives us the first vision of the ideal we hope to reach, but without the mind, we will never see how to get there. Thus, there is a place for both the light of faith and the light of the mind; both must be cultivated and used for the purposes they are designed to fulfill.

It is the light of the mind, transmitting the light of the soul, which makes us a worthy companion of God and other divine beings. To leave the mind undeveloped is to remain on the outer fringes of humanity, in partial darkness. To train the mind and apply it to life is to enter into the full light of day, the full glory of being a proper son or daughter of God.

In this full illumination at the end of our journey, the crystal lens is ultimately revealed to be a diamond with eight facets. These eight facets are right action, right direction, right attitude, right thought, right speech, right recollection, right meditation, and right work. Through them, our light shines into the world.

Through the mature and perfected mind, we find God, serve God, and reveal God. The mind, therefore, is more than just a lens for the soul; in its completeness, it is a beam of light connecting heaven with earth.

COPING WITH STRESS

Each of us carries throughout life assorted bundles and burdens of duty, work, and expectation which periodically weigh us down with stress and conflict. We are not meant to suffer excessively from these burdens, however, but rather see them as ingredients of change, spurring us on to become a better person. The key is learning to turn within and discover the peace of the inner self, which can lighten our load and enlighten our way.

A MASTER OF CIRCUMSTANCE

One of the great masterpieces of American art is *Voyage of Life,* a series of four canvases by the nineteenth century painter Thomas Cole. In this work, Cole allegorically captures the hopes, aspirations, and struggles of mankind and vividly states his belief that in spite of the obstacles and stress to be faced in life, each of us does succeed in discovering and expressing some part of our transcendent greatness. Cole obviously had deep insight into the plights we confront and the peace we can achieve if we persevere. In the first canvas, "Childhood," a newborn infant emerges in a small, golden boat from the cavern of birth, filled with dawning promise and unaware of any difficulties ahead. Next, in "Youth," the infant has grown into a young man who idealistically pursues his vision of life. The vision in the sky is bright and shining and seems, to the youth, to be all he needs to guide him on his voyage along the tributaries of earth. From it he derives a sense of peace, but it is an insubstantial peace, soon to be shattered on the yet unseen rapids around the bend. In the third canvas, "Manhood," the idealism of the youth is sorely tested by all the stress, opposition, and conflict of adulthood. His golden boat seems tiny now and not stable enough to withstand the rushing currents which relentlessly propel him forward, nor the mighty winds that rock him from side to side. All seems dark; his vision has vanished and with it his illusory sense of tranquillity. Frightened, despairing, and lonely, he prays for release from his trials. This deliverance comes in the fourth panel, "Old Age," when the matured man emerges from the turmoil of life with a new understanding and awareness. To some, it might appear he has been defeated: his boat is severely damaged and stands becalmed in a large lake. But this is not the case: although his barque is battered, his spirit has triumphed. The heavens open wide, pouring forth a magnificent light upon the earth. Both his vision of youth and his prayer of adulthood are fulfilled; he has overcome his struggles. In so doing, he has gained wisdom and achieved stability; he is ready to approach the kingdom of heaven and learn the secret of divine peace.

Like the voyager in Cole's painting, we all yearn for peace, but must deal instead with stress, conflict, and imperfection. Most of us do not invite this discord into our lives, yet it comes anyway. It sneaks in through our relationships, our petty irritations, the pressures of work, our battles with time, our insecurities and embarrassments, the fears and worries of mass consciousness, our failures—and even our expectations and triumphs! Stress is an inevitable element of life—not an enjoyable element, but one we must learn to cope with wisely.

Strife is inherent in life itself, a necessary ingredient in change, growth, and achievement. It can be found in the upheavals of nature, the territorial instincts of animals, the cycles of the economy, and the dealings of groups and nations, as well as in individual attitudes and circumstances. A person without stress is either still a child—or dead.

Few people, however, understand stress and the role it plays in accomplishment and growth. They simply know that they do not care for it, and try to avoid it as adroitly as they can. It is not possible, however, to escape stress and conflict — and the effort to do so is likely to produce far more frustration and unhappiness than the original conditions of discord! Stress cannot be wished out of existence; the only effective way of coping with it is to acknowledge, understand, and conquer it. The artist of life therefore accepts stress as a fundamental principle of human activity.

The acceptance of stress as a part of life, however, does not include the glorification of it. Some people attempt to deal with stress by submitting passively to it, letting it rule their lives and believing that the perception of acute pain somehow makes them more alive, more human. The glorification of stress is just as absurd as the attempt to avoid it. Discord and tension are genuine factors in the human condition, but they are not meant to be our masters. Quite the contrary: *we are meant to master them!* Instead of resigning to conflict, we are supposed to wrestle with it and learn to harmonize the elements of discord. Rather than enduring chaos, we are meant to impose order where it is lacking in our life, and thereby set the stage for peace. Far from succumbing to imperfection, we are supposed to rise above it and reform it.

But before we can master stress, we will have to understand what produces it, why people react negatively to it, and how it can be tamed and transmuted into a creative force. To succeed in this endeavor, we will have to be willing to set aside popular ideas and prejudices about stress, and approach it objectively. We must especially resist the temptation to blame others or society for our stress! The act of blaming others is nothing but a retreat into ignorance and blindness.

To understand what produces stress, we need to learn about the esoteric principle of "the pairs of opposites." According to this principle, the emergence of any idea, plan, or impulse into manifestation leads inevitably to a duality. As this duality becomes defined, it creates opposite extremes. Through the interaction of these opposite extremes, a dynamic tension is established, inducing—sooner or later—action, growth, and the reconciliation of the extremes.

As a result, there is a significant relationship between the seeming opposites of conflict and harmony, chaos and peace, and imperfection and perfection. Conflict arises where there is a lack of harmony; harmony is created by mastering conflict and establishing balance in the conditions of life. Chaos is the absence of peace; peace is achieved by imposing order on chaotic circumstances. Imperfection is unfinished perfection; perfection is attained by striving to complete our evolutionary journey. Harmony, peace, and perfection are all more desirable than their polar opposites, but to be sensible, we must realize that they cannot be achieved without enduring some tension and stress. We will experience much conflict before we master harmony; we will suffer much chaos before we discover the full power of peace; we will be exposed to much imperfection before we learn to create perfection. The interaction of the pairs of opposites guarantees it.

Indeed, if we pray for peace, our prayer will often be answered by increased conflict and stress—giving us the opportunity to improve our skills as a peacemaker. If we invoke harmony, the response is likely to come in the form of greater discord—forcing us to act with increased harmony. And as we cry out for perfection, we become more painfully aware of the imperfection in our own life which needs our attention. Should we become bogged down in reacting to the unpleasant aspects of these conditions, we would not learn our lessons and evolve. But if we realize that the negative pole of stress can be connected to the positive pole of peace, thereby producing balance, we can neutralize the unpleasantness. In fact, we can greatly enrich our life, with new power, sanity, order, reason, and idealism.

The principle of the pairs of opposites therefore also explains the reason why most people react so negatively to stress. Not understanding the value of the tension between the opposite extremes, and the creative opportunity for growth and productivity it provides, they respond to it on a purely emotional level. They allow themselves to be threatened by imperfection, irritated by chaos, and upset by conflict. It should be understood, however, that there is nothing *inherently* threatening about imperfection, annoying about chaos, and upsetting about conflict. It is just as reasonable to expect each of these conditions to inspire us to act and strengthen our will to achieve. The fact that they seldom do is merely an indication of how frequently most of us permit our emotions to dominate our attitudes and thinking about life.

And yet, the attitude with which we confront stress and disharmony is *the single most crucial factor* determining our success in coping with these problems. We have no choice in whether or not we will experience chaos and conflict—they are generated by the pairs of opposites. But we do have a choice as to *how we react* to the struggles of life.

There are two basic options—"Plan A" and "Plan B." Most of us choose Plan A, in which we register great anguish, pain, and despair. We become obsessed with our weaknesses and paranoid about recurrent problems, thereby adding new stress to old and undermining our peace of mind, emotional stability, and physical health. We fear the worst, worry about improbabilities, and exaggerate the dimensions of our problems until they are so large that they overwhelm us. Finally, having become desperate and abject, we bitterly complain that life has not treated us fairly.

But it need not be so. We can also choose Plan B, in which we respond to chaotic and threatening conditions with an inner peace and sense of dignity which enable us to act confidently and efficiently to correct the worst of the difficulties we face—or, at the very least, minimize their unfortunate consequences. The strength of Plan B is that it places the emphasis on taking action to resolve the problems at hand, not just become hysterical or despondent. It represents an affirmative step toward reducing the magnitude of the problem, invoking help, and discovering the potential for growth inherent in the dilemma we face.

When a person who operates under the influence of Plan A is plunged into a stressful situation, he quickly begins thinking of himself as a victim of forces beyond his control. As a result, he paralyzes his capacity to act. But the person guided by Plan B responds in a completely different way, by assessing the options before him, examining what he can do to correct the difficulty, and then acting with quiet confidence. He emerges as a master of circumstance, not a slave to it.

One of the most common causes of stress, for example, is embarrassment, where we have been careless or thoughtless or possibly even unethical. Occasional embarrassment is part of the human condition—no one can escape it, because we all make mistakes. But we do have a choice as to how stressful these moments of embarrassment will be. If we are a Plan A person, they will be devastating. We will privately chastise ourself for being so stupid or foolish as to make the mistake, but will publicly blame others for not warning us in time, or for tempting us in the first place, or even for having the audacity to expose our pecadillo and cause such great embarrassment. Having made one mistake, we now compound it with another, by reacting absurdly and childishly to the embarrassment we have brought on ourself. This is the way stress builds.

The Plan B person, by contrast, keeps the embarrassment in perspective. He apologizes to those he may have hurt, acts to rectify the damage done, and then proceeds with more important matters—without being rattled, ruffled, or rumpled emotionally by the incident. He may even find it possible to convert the embarrassment into an opportunity for growth, by expressing dignity, good humor, and humility while making amends. In this way, he adds strength to his character.

The difference between Plan A and Plan B lies in the nature of our *reaction* to stressful events and circumstance. In Plan A, we react emotionally, and magnify the event beyond its rightful significance. In Plan B, we respond mentally, trying to understand what has gone awry and act intelligently to correct it. Neither plan eliminates suffering or stress from our life—it just represents one of two ways of coping with it. Obviously, Plan B is the more intelligent of the two—although the less commonly used.

By understanding this fundamental distinction, it

becomes possible to see how stress can be tamed and transmuted into a creative force. The key, strangely enough, lies in our approach to "suffering."

Suffering is the act of recognizing that something is wrong or imperfect and needs correction. It is a necessary and healthy part of life, for how else can the spiritual person perceive the work to be done, the imperfection to be corrected? Suffering motivates us to become more skilled and involved in the process of living. But it is highly important that *we control* the process of suffering. If we do not, it will quickly control us.

Ideally, the grip of suffering is intended to last just long enough to enable us to perceive the deficiency or problem at hand. For a skilled observer of life, a moment should be sufficient. Then, our better nature should take control and respond to our suffering with competence and strength, correcting the imperfection as best we can. Instead of becoming grief-stricken and hysterical, we act peacefully, calmly. This is the goal of Plan B: to suffer in a spiritual sense yet still know peace, so that we can work harmoniously with our spiritual ideals to impose order on chaos, resolution on difficulty.

The problem with Plan A, by contrast, is that it makes the act of suffering into an emotional *cause célèbre*. Instead of being an objective, detached perception of what is wrong and needs repairing, suffering becomes a prolonged reaction of hysteria, agony, panic, grief, or depression to our misfortunes. We lose control of the act of suffering and are overwhelmed by feelings of distress.

Some people believe this latter type of suffering, in which we torment ourself with conflict and discord, to be an important part of human life; if we are not suffering emotionally, they claim, we are not really alive. This argument, however, is usually set forth as an unwitting justification for complacency and immature behavior in the face of conflict. Reacting to life in accordance with Plan A is a masochistic luxury we can ill afford. It is not the heroic struggle its proponents suppose it to be, but more the pathetic agony of self-professed martyrs.

Life does not force us to agonize in our suffering; instead, it subtly encourages us to meet our stress and conflict with courage and harmony. It rewards our efforts to rise above our emotional reactiveness and deal intelligently with *all* opportunities for growth which come to us—not just the ones we deem favorable. It helps us mature and supports us as we try to identify with the state of peace which is a natural part of the life of our higher self.

Correctly managed, suffering helps us *transmute* stress into peace, correcting mistakes where they are found and lessening the impact of hardship where it occurs, but always with a measure of detachment and poise. It replaces emotional agony with intelligent activity, enabling us to solve problems and impose order on chaos. As we do, we discover the true meaning of peace. Peace is the ability to work with a vast number of factors, both pleasant and unpleasant with such harmony and efficiency that we incur no stress or discomfort. Peace is a dynamic state of great activity which impels us to fulfill our highest ideals and recognize our responsibilities to one another—and to life itself.

This is a point worth reflecting on, because peace is commonly believed to be a state of stillness or deadness, in which there is an utter absence of all activity, difficulty, or conflict. We refer to people who have died as "resting in peace" and to people who are asleep as "sleeping as peacefully as a baby." We define world peace as an absence of warfare, rather than an active state of cooperation. A "peaceful night" is one in which nothing happens. Gurus from the East encourage us to discover "spiritual peace" by emptying our minds, staring blankly at a candle or mumbling a meaningless mantra, and doing nothing. Modern psychologists prescribe physical relaxation as the most important element in therapies for coping with stress.

These are unfortunate distortions of the true power of peace. Peace is not stillness! It is not deadness! It is not emptiness! Nor is it a state of rest or relaxation. It is a dynamic ability to act with poise, confidence, and effectiveness. Stillness is an illusion which can only be achieved and sustained by a flight into fantasy. Deadness is a regressive withdrawal into a state of isolation which walls us off from the mainstream of evolution. Emptiness is a denial of the principle of abundance and fulfillment, a form of psychological suicide.

Peace, by contrast, is the byproduct of learning to manage our daily affairs with skill, efficiency, and the guidance of the inner self. It is a dynamic capacity for confronting conflict and stress and imposing order on chaos. It is never found by retreating from stress, but by plunging into it and learning to solve problems, direct powerful forces, and produce meaningful results. Peace is not so much an ideal as it is an inner state of thought and attitude.

Being an inner state of thought and attitude, neither the creation nor the duration of peace is dependent upon peaceful-appearing conditions in our environment. An individual can be caught up in a natural disaster such as a hurricane or an earthquake and still act with peace—calmly and courageously responding to the emergency and supporting others. A company can be threatened by bitter competitiveness or a harsh economy and still respond peacefully—by increasing its productivity, achieving greater internal harmony, and putting more emphasis on the service it gives to the general public. A nation can be thrust into circumstances of war and nevertheless maintain a measure of genuine peace—its citizens responding with self-sacrifice and purpose, the government acting with constitutional integrity, and the public as a whole rising to meet the challenge of the hour.

One of the great examples of peace, in fact, can be found in the life of Abraham Lincoln. Throughout his life, Lincoln knew he was a man of destiny, designed to fill a noble and heroic purpose. And yet, until he was elected President, his efforts to fulfill that destiny were frustrated, because the moment of his great opportunity had not arrived. Being unable to act on his purpose, Lincoln was not at peace with himself, even though his life included a number of successes and significant popularity. Once he became President, however, his inner frustration ceased—not because of the fame or power he had acquired but because he knew he was now fulfilling his destiny! He acquired the only genuine peace he knew during his lifetime, and this in spite of the fact that the whole country was plunged into a civil war. Chaos surrounded him on all sides, and Lincoln surely suffered greatly from it. He was a highly sensitive and compassionate individual, responsive to the pain of women who had lost sons and husbands in the war and keenly aware of the damage being done. But he was a strong person who was able to respond to suffering with peace, an inner peace born of the conviction that a noble purpose was being served—that the suffering was not in vain. It was this peace which enabled Lincoln to hold the nation together and reunite it; it was this peace that provided a platform for his ideal of "malice toward none; with charity for all; with firmness in the right, as God gives us to see the right."

It is this kind of dynamic peace which truly makes us a master of circumstance, in command of stress and tension, never a slave to them. The ability to approach life peacefully is therefore one of the great skills of the art of living. It is rooted in our innermost spirit and capacity for growth—the wisdom, strength, and love of the center of our being—but like any skill, we acquire peacefulness only as we understand it, cultivate it, practice it, and achieve competence in expressing it. *Merely praying for peace is not enough to create peaceful conditions!* Our prayers must be accompanied by constructive action of our own. We must use the measure of peace we discover within to heal the imperfections and deficiencies of our life, our environment, our nation, and humanity as a whole.

The time for suffering in anguish and allowing stress to dominate us has passed. It is time to learn to use the act of suffering to perceive imperfection and opposition and then act promptly and responsibly to correct and heal these conditions, wherever they arise.

It is time to herald the value of *peace in the midst of suffering.*

THE INGREDIENTS OF CHANGE

In Shakespeare's words, "All the world's a stage, and all the men and women merely players." The artist of life knows, however, that the drama being performed on this grand stage is not exactly what it seems to be. It is a drama of consciousness—a play which is constantly being rewritten, revised, improved, and perfected, so that consciousness can unfold and achieve better expression. Most of the action of the play does not even occur on earth—it occurs in heaven, through the interaction of divine archetypes and other elements of spirit. But as consciousness itself expands and grows, there is a corresponding expansion and growth in the character and behavior of the players.

This phenomenon produces a constant flow of plans, ideals, and forces from heaven to earth, as new directions of growth filter slowly into the conscious awareness of humanity. It is therefore reasonable to expect that change and growth will be two of the most significant factors in our life. But wherever there is change, we must also expect to find a certain measure of inertia—a resistance to change which prefers the status quo and will fight to preserve it. This resistance to growth can be found in the human personality, in groups, and in society as a whole. And, when inertia comes head-to-head with the thrust of evolution, the result is conflict.

The struggle between resistance and growth—between what has been and what is to come, between the outer and the inner dimensions of life—is the heart of all conflict and stress. It is the struggle between heaven and earth. And, because the members of the human race are the players of this grand drama, we are constantly exposed to this fundamental conflict.

If we understand the benefits and growth which come out of conflict, we can handle our predicament reasonably well and even find a working measure of peace. But if we fail to grasp the noble purpose and ultimate result of the discord we must face, it is all too easy to identify excessively with it, falling victim to stress, discouragement, hysteria, and despair. We may even cast our lot in favor of resistance and inertia, clinging stubbornly to the outer forms of life. Not comprehending the evolving nature of life, we dream of putting a stop to the threat of change.

In order for growth to occur there must always be a gap between the ideal state of things and the actual state of things, just as there must always be positive and negative charges in a magnetic field to produce electrical current. And since growth is a constant factor in life, then obviously there will always be a certain amount of disparity and difference between the opposite poles we face: between the transcendent and the mundane, the potential and the manifest, our innate talent and the way we use it, and our aspirations and what we actually do. If we overemphasize this disparity, we are likely to suffer acutely. But if we try to ignore it, we will stagnate. The challenge, therefore, is to grow without being overwhelmed by the stress which is a necessary part of growth—and that requires a well-developed sense of balance.

The balanced person is one who can see both poles of disparity at the same time and recognize the value of each, without being ruled by either. He treads a middle course which harnesses the power of the conflict between the extremes, instead of giving in to it. He is able, for example, to balance the need for active involvement in the mundane concerns of life with the need for thoughtful reflection upon and obedience to the transcendent values and ethics of life. It is not always easy to achieve the ideal level of balance in the conflicts we face, however. There are several factors to consider:

• The goal is growth, not the attainment of absolute perfection. The perfectionist who cannot tolerate even the smallest error invites great turmoil which others are not troubled by. An obsession with perfection is an unbalanced condition. Perfection should always be the ideal we strive toward—but never the criterion for evaluating our performance. Success lies far more in *growing toward* perfection than in actually achieving total flawlessness.

- The process of growth requires great patience. If we are impatient with ourself, with others, and with life in general, we will incur much discord. In this regard, it is always wise to keep in mind that the work of evolution is an ongoing process, one in which we have been involved for millions of years. There is still much to do—but an enormous amount has already been accomplished. The fact that progress occasionally seems slow is not an indication of failure—it is primarily a sign that we do not fully appreciate the larger scope of evolution. Impatience knocks us off balance. Patience restores it.

- There are certain restrictions of time, talent, and resources which every human being must understand and take into account. The person who takes on more work or responsibilities than he can possibly manage—through bad judgment, vanity, or greed—is sure to create conditions of personal distress. Balance is not achieved, however, by deliberately taking on *less* work than we can manage! It is attained by honestly matching the time, talent, and resources potentially available to us with the work and responsibilities we commit ourself to.

- We must be willing to grow and experiment with life. If we are unwilling to take necessary risks and put our talents and skills "on the line," we will soon discover how much stress can be created by reluctance and hesitation.

- Not all factors contributing to stress are easily discerned. Frequently, the higher self has a different objective in mind than the personality. But the will of the higher self tends to be stronger, in most situations, than the will of the personality. As conditions unfold, they may well appear undesirable to the personality—and yet be in perfect harmony with the intentions of the inner being. An important part of achieving balance, therefore, is understanding that the personality lives and moves and has its being as an integral part of a large whole.

- Many of the factors of stress are beyond our personal control, generated as a result of our dealings with others, the environment, and the larger forces of human life. In such instances, balance must be maintained by remaining nonreactive, detached. It is pointless, for example, to become irritated and annoyed simply because someone else is in a bad mood and is letting it influence his behavior toward us. But most of us do! We lose our sense of balance. Nor is it sensible to react to changes in the weather as though they were personal insults intended just to upset our plans—or to changes in the economy, or politics, or the life of the nation.

Balance is not a juggling act, in which we try to see how many rubber balls we can keep in the air at one time, without letting any of them fall. It is an important technique of growth, a way of harmonizing the inner ideal with the current conditions of life. Balance harnesses the tension of stress, making it useful, instead of dissipating it. When the power of balance is understood, we begin to see that stress is not meant to be a life-and-death struggle. Conflict is not a war between incompatible extremes; it is the friction which arises naturally between heaven and earth as the process of growth presses on inexorably toward the mark.

The challenge of handling stress is meant to be something like growing wheat and transforming it into bread for our table. In order to grow, the wheat must endure the burning summer sun, the threat of flooding from torrential downpours, weeds which try to choke it out, and insects intent on devouring it. When it is mature, the wheat must be harvested, threshed, and processed into flour. The flour is then mixed with other ingredients to form a sticky goo, kneaded violently, and baked in the fierce heat of an oven. If the wheat could be consciously aware of these steps, it would undoubtedly groan miserably about its neverending suffering. "That fellow Job in the Bible had an easy time of it," the wheat would say. "He should have been a loaf of bread. Then he would have known true misery!" We, of course, can objectively see that the stress involved in each step of becoming bread is more apparent than real; indeed, the benefits obtained can be gained in no other way. Wheat cannot be magically transformed into bread without intervening effort; the necessary changes must evolve step by step, until the process is completed.

We, too, are figuratively being "harvested, threshed, and kneaded" — by our own inner being. We are being prepared for a noble destiny, even though we lose sight of this fact at times. To maintain balance, we should embrace this destiny and accept its implication — that we will periodically have to experience phases of imperfection and discomfort in order to grow and fulfill the plans of the higher self. We should strive to see conflict and stress as *the ingredients of change,* not as threats. They are signs that some important transformation or transmutation is in progress, and while we may not be able to see exactly what the final goal is, we can be confident it is worthwhile. By its very nature, conflict is designed to lead eventually to harmony. Imperfection is likewise meant to lead to perfection, chaos to peace. We are not engaged in battles between the forces of darkness and light, or wars between spirit and matter. We are involved in a meaningful process of closing the gaps of disparity which separate earth from heaven. We are part of the work of harmonizing and harnessing the ingredients of change—in our own life and in the affairs of society.

It would be an overstatement to claim that there is *value* in conflict and stress, but it is certainly helpful to regard these ingredients of change as useful parts of life. While the world we live in does contain chaotic conditions and harmful events, we should never assume that chaos and injury exist only to antagonize us and make us miserable. Life is *not* irrational. We are not pitched against insuperable odds, doomed to a life of frustration and failure. Quite the contrary: we live in an orderly universe, designed to evolve and expand, and therefore moving through various stages of imperfection. The conflict resulting from this natural unfoldment is meant to *stir up* the life within and around us, and within nations, civilization, and the institutions of society, too. This is a beneficial process. After all, an individual who has no conflict to face soon becomes "fat and sassy," making little effort to grow or mature. The same can be observed in business monopolies which have no competition and government bureaucracies which are allowed to operate unchecked. To government bureaucracies and protected monopolies, citizen watchdog groups which hound them for poor performance are sources of great stress, conflict, and pain. But for the rest of us, these groups serve a valuable role in helping to maintain effective government and public services. They represent the constructive side of stress and conflict.

For the individual, the constructive side of conflict includes a number of significant benefits:

1. It forces us to become more efficient and trim away our excess fat—to discard our "useless baggage." It is helpful to be stirred up in this way periodically, just as moving to a new home every few years, while unsettling, nonetheless serves the purpose of helping us avoid being overwhelmed by our possessions. Invariably, as we pack up to move, we discover that many of the items we have stored away in our closets and drawers are no longer useful to us. In fact, they could have been thrown away, given away, or sold long ago; now we have the perfect opportunity to get rid of them. Moments of crisis and conflict in our personal life serve much the same function. They help us lighten our burden, so we will not be buried by outdated habits, worn-out attitudes, and useless prejudices and ideas. They force us to streamline our consciousness by redefining our goals, values, and lifestyle. And they require us to focus on the major issues of life, instead of being distracted by the minor pettiness which so often catches our attention.

2. Conflict frequently encourages us to search in the deeper levels of our humanity and discover our spiritual strengths, wisdom, courage, talents, endurance, and patience, so that we may better cope with and overcome the challenges life presents to us. There are times in life when we are pushed to the very brink of our competence by stress and crisis, only to realize that this outer limit of skill and ability is no longer enough. We must become even stronger, more courageous, more loving, or more intelligent than before.

We do not quite know how to attain what we need, but we seek it nonetheless. In response, our innermost spiritual powers come to us and lift us beyond our limitations to a new height of achievement, power, or love. This type of growth is often the underlying purpose of family or business crises. When first confronted with the problem, we wonder how we will cope. But as we strive to remain calm, we find we are able to make rapid and accurate decisions, assign duties to others, and lead the family or business out of the miserable strife it is in. For a period of time, we become absolutely heroic in what we are and what we do. The crisis soon passes, but the new strength, wisdom, and endurance do not. These qualities remain as a constant part of our character.

3. In dealing with conflict, we are also given ideal opportunities for recognizing the hidden laws of life which govern change, and the characteristics of evolution in our own life. If we reflect upon the different types of conflict and stress we have experienced, for instance, we can begin to see patterns of circumstance which reveal the nature of our individual destiny and duty. In the same way, if we muse upon the patterns of conflict which have occurred in business, society, or the nation, we can start to understand something of the inner direction involved. These patterns often are presented to us quite forcefully. After all, if we are a selfish and demanding person who exploits others and treats life dishonestly, we are not apt to mend our ways just on the suggestion of a friend who points out our shortcomings. Indeed, we will probably tell him to mind his own affairs. But if over and over again we strike up relationships with other people who are even more selfish and demanding than we are—people who can defeat us at our own game—then eventually we

will realize the value of changing our ways. The frustration and self-pity which will accumulate from being repeatedly victimized will at some point become too much to bear, and it will finally dawn on us that the universe does not support our selfishness and dishonesty. We will begin to understand that it is impossible to fool the universe, and thus set about becoming a more responsible and caring individual.

It is in exactly the same way that groups of people and nations frequently learn their lessons as well. After a selfish, separative group has been persecuted, scorned, and rejected often enough, it slowly learns to be a better member of the human family. After a nation has tolerated dictatorial and totalitarian rulers long enough, it gradually resolves to respect the rights of its individual citizens, safeguard its freedoms, and prevent the imposition of tyranny. The suffering which must be experienced before these lessons are learned is often quite intense, because a whole mass of people has to be stirred to action, not just one individual. Yet conflict and stress are usually the only motivating forces most people heed.

4. Because conflict and stress must be faced by all members of humanity alike, our own experiences with suffering help us appreciate that other people suffer, too. This, too, is a benefit of conflict, as it helps us understand we are our brother's keeper; we are all part of a vast fellowship called humanity, and we need to take care of one another.

If we are already motivated to help others, the lessons we learn from conflict can underscore the value of focusing our efforts effectively. By discovering that peace and freedom from pain are inner states, for example, we come to understand that just removing the external causes of strife is never enough to eliminate suffering. Often, it simply intensifies the dependency of the needy on others. And so, instead of mindlessly giving money to help the downtrodden, we learn to truly care about the plight of others and to share with them the strength and love which can transform their lives.

On the other hand, if we have not previously cared that much about serving our fellow voyagers through life, the discord and trauma we experience through our own conflict will gradually open our eyes to the impact we can have — and do have — on others. As we suffer from the careless words and thoughtless omissions of others, we learn to speak carefully and thoughtfully ourself — to praise others when they deserve it, to support them when they need it. As we miss opportunities through the lack of cooperation from others, we learn the need to be helpful ourself, so that others will not miss opportunities and suffer as we have suffered. In these ways, our humanity warms up and we become more compassionate, caring, and involved. Once hardnosed and tough-minded, our direct experience of personal tragedy humbles us and makes us much more human — more caring and quicker to offer compliments, praise, and sympathy. Instead of scorning the weak, whose threshold for suffering is less than ours, we realize that everyone has his own individual susceptibility to stress and pain. And so we accept the weaknesses of others without indulging them — and try to help them as best we can. In this way, our own acquaintance with hardship inspires us to serve others.

5. Above all, conflict forces us to improve the quality and competence of our personality — our ability to act in daily life. It makes us become more productive and a better agent for the love, strengths, qualities, and

plans of our innermost spirit. By coping with conflict, we gradually see what is imperfect in our life and how it can be corrected. Having to solve a lot of problems, for example, may be unpleasant while it is going on, but it will train us to become a good problem solver. This, in turn, will open up new opportunites for success in our work and our personal life. Discovering our inefficiencies and carelessness may cause us great pain for awhile, but once we have corrected the deficiencies and have become efficient and careful, the anguish disappears. We realize that our pain was worthwhile after all. Just so, if we are confronted with vicious prejudice and persecuted by cruel people, we may experience great suffering and perhaps even death. But to the degree that we acquire greater endurance, steadfastness, mercifulness, and genuine righteousness, we triumph over the taunts and tortures of our malicious opponents.

Indeed, whatever the nature of the conflict we personally experience, we learn something about being a peacemaker. To overcome internal stress, such as worry or fear or self-pity, we must learn to establish peace with ourself. To overcome external stress, caused by others, we must learn to make peace with them — not by surrendering, but by creating relationships which honor our mutual ideals. To overcome the stress of a group or nation, we must learn to create an atmosphere of peace which advances the purpose of the group.

These are the constructive roles of conflict. In large and small measures, they come to us every day. If we respond selfishly and foolishly to them, we negate most of the potential growth we might tap. If we glorify stress and make a cult out of suffering, we distort its purpose and harm our well-being. But if we make an honest effort to cope with stress wisely and use it constructively in the art of living, then conflict can be a building block upon which we establish efficiency, strength, wisdom, service, and competence.

In fact, it can represent the cutting edge of personal growth and enlightened change in our life.

THE CENTER OF ACTION

The greatest danger in working with stress and conflict is to become too immersed in the difficulties they represent. It is extremely easy to let a problem or a threat become the center of our attention, to the point where our thoughts and emotions are saturated by it. When this is allowed to happen, however, we become hypnotized by the strength of the difficulty; we begin to believe there is no solution, no recourse. We start defining everything in life in relation to our problem.

If we are to cope wisely with stress, we must never become a slave to it, or let it dominate our attention. On the contrary, we should discipline ourself to shift our attention away from the problem at hand as often as possible, focusing it instead on our capacity to solve this difficulty. In this regard, we should never forget that the purpose of conflict is to motivate us to create conditions of harmony and peace in our life. We suffer only so that we will be inspired to correct the cause of our suffering.

The proper response to stress and conflict, therefore, is to flood our awareness with a strong sense of peace. But before this is possible, we must have a clear understanding of what peace is. The usual popular ideas about peace will not suffice, however; they have done far more to injure the cause of peace than promote it. What we need is a blueprint or model of peace we can work from—a model based on the divine archetypal patterns known to our inner self. Then, guided by this model, we must strive to reproduce the essence of peace as faithfully as we can in our own attitudes, feelings, and thoughts. If we do, we will slowly generate within our subconscious a reservoir of peace which is connected in turn with the infinite resources of peace in the universe. When this connection is fully established, the presence of peace within us will be unshakeable.

For an individual, peace comes by expressing the inherent order and perfection of God's life through intelligent activity. This order and perfection exist at the level of the soul and can be tapped in quiet moments of reflection or contemplation. But it only becomes active in our life as we begin approaching the activities of daily life with attitudes, thoughts, and moods which are in harmony with this essence of order and perfection. Only as we bring heaven to earth and put it to work in our lifestyle and productive roles do we establish peace on earth for ourself.

A group or nation attains peace in similar ways, by expressing the order and perfection of God through its activities, institutions, and conduct. As in the case of the individual, this order and perfection exist at the archetypal level—in the inner spirit of the group or nation. Yet it will remain only a hope for the future until the members of the group or nation begin to act in harmony with these inner ideals, even in the face of stress.

Peace requires active involvement in life, not stillness. It is a mistake to think of peace in the context of resting, as any truly active person knows. The active person finds it impossible to stop his activity and do absolutely nothing. He begins to fidget and look for something to do. Indeed, to the active person, inactivity brings great stress. It shatters the genuine sense of peace he is able to establish while working. This is not to imply that there is no value in relaxing; relaxation is an important part of refreshing the human mechanism and preparing it for more activity. *But stopping and becoming absolutely still destroys true peace!*

Peace is the essence of stability within the heart of any noble activity, the center of dynamic action in any form or event. It is a nucleus of direction, power, and purpose within a larger whole. In many ways, in fact, it can be compared to the life of the atom. Physics teaches us that the atom is a unit of energy with a stable nucleus and peripheral elements which move in relationship to this center. Within the atom there is intense activity; at times the form of the atom even changes to a degree, going to a higher energy state or a different isotope. But these changes occur in an orderly and peaceful way; the atom continues to fulfill its purpose and function in spite of them. Furthermore, its nature and identity remain essentially the same. In these ways, the features of the atom embody the nature of peace. Like the nucleus, peace is the stable center of life which regulates the orderly flow of activities on the periphery. It operates in the midst of great activity but remains a constant factor. While the outer form of its expression easily changes, it nonetheless endures, imparting a sense of stability and identity to the individual, group, or nation that works with it.

Other analogies can also give us ideas of the nature of peace—for example, the mathematical principle that two plus two equals four. This is a formula which can be used reliably to produce meaningful results. It does not wear down or fall apart; indeed, it is the "keystone" holding the whole system of addition together. This basic principle can be used by millions of people simultaneously — even hysterical, panicky, or fearful people. It survives the mistakes of grade-school children and careless adults. And as it is used, it gives order and structure to our calculations and accounts. Peace behaves in much the same way. As we act with peace in our life, we set the stage for meaningful accomplishment. We draw to us conditions and opportunities which augment our chances for achievement. We discover that peace preserves us from chaos and confusion; no matter how distressed the people or conditions around us become, our inner peace does not falter — if it is genuine. And, by acting with peace, we come to understand that there is structure and purpose in life.

Any mechanical device which works efficiently also makes a good model for the nature of peace. An automobile, for example, is a good analogy for the way peace should operate in a national group. The automobile is a machine composed of many complex parts, all of which must function as they are designed to and when they are supposed to, if it is to fulfill its purpose. Just so, the citizens of a country must recognize and fulfill their individual responsibilities, if the whole nation is to operate peacefully. The automobile is meant to be used actively, but within certain restraints. It is to be driven on highways, for example, and not on open pastures or lakes. Similarly, the peace of a nation depends on active cooperation with other nations in commerce, tourism, culture, and diplomacy; a nation which tries to isolate itself will incur stress instead of building peace. Furthermore, in driving a car we are expected to observe traffic laws and not collide with other vehicles. In much the same way, the peace of a nation depends on respecting the integrity and sovereignty of other countries. When an automobile fulfills its design and is driven properly, it operates peacefully. When it is neglected or abused the efficiency of its operation is quickly lost. The same can be postulated for the peace of nations.

Perhaps the best model for peace at work within the world about us, though, is the ecological structure of nature and the ability of each individual plant or animal to adapt to it. Somehow the whole of nature is harmonious and able to evolve, even though the individual parts are quite different one from the other — and sometimes in conflict. There is a central force in nature, called life, which keeps the whole system in balance, uses timed cycles to temporarily end growth and then renew it in spring, and causes the right plants or life forms to grow in the correct place at the proper time, so that balance is maintained. In this manner, nature operates in an orderly fashion, with rhythm. It does not tolerate chaos or imperfection, but slowly works to remove them through the process of natural selection.

Man can learn much about working peacefully by interacting with nature, God's great example of peace. By learning to work with the laws of botany, for instance, we come to appreciate the thoughtfulness and intelligence behind this creation. We learn how to make changes within an orderly system without upsetting the order — how to create more productive plants, strains that are more resistant to disease, and soil conditions which will help the plants grow. Luther Burbank and George Washington Carver are outstanding examples of human beings who were able to work peacefully with the secrets and powers of nature.

It is interesting, in this regard, that much is made these days of the ability of the American Indians to be in tune with nature and at peace with the plants, animals, rivers, and skies. To a degree this is true, but it has been overstated in our eagerness to romanticize a part of our heritage. The Indians actually did little to interact with nature. Their cultivation of the land was primitive; their understanding of the laws of nature was more defensive than creative. It is therefore a bit off the mark to view them as being *at peace* with nature, except in the inactive, stilled sense of peace. It would be more accurate to say they were passively in awe of nature. It is people such as Burbank and Carver who are truly at peace with nature.

The atom, mathematics, the automobile, and nature are just a few of the many models which demonstrate, by analogy and application, the nature of peace. By learning from them the role peace plays as the *center of action*, we can gradually shift our attention away from the stress and difficulties which upset us, and focus it on our inner potential to master and transform our problems. We can build up, in our character, the qualities and strengths we need to become an agent of peace and resolve the chaotic conditions which have plagued us.

As we do, we set the stage for becoming at peace with ourself.

ASSETS IN LIVING

As we identify with the peace of our inner self, and seek to express it in the constant activity of daily life, we gradually learn to handle any degree of stress and conflict. But if we try to cope with turmoil *without* pursuing first the ideal of peace, we will simply augment the burdens which weigh upon us. Without the stable center of peace to rely on, our actions are far more likely to *add* chaos and confusion to our problems, not lessen them.

Unfortunately, few people know the value of cultivating a genuine capacity to work peacefully. Most of us look instead for an easy-to-use, magical formula which will miraculously cause our woes and anxieties to vanish, leaving no trace. There are many magical formulas that we try — but none of them works.

The most common magical formula is the disappearing act — we try to avoid the source of stress or conflict. If we have an unpleasant job, for instance, we quit and seek employment elsewhere, rather than try to understand why we dislike it and how we can change our attitudes and become more at peace with the opportunities at hand. If we dislike the city we live in, we move to a different one, instead of attempting to understand the advantages and benefits of living there. If we quarrel with our neighbors, we ignore them socially, instead of searching for ways to improve the relationship. If we have an unsatisfying relationship, we get a divorce or seek satisfaction elsewhere. Or, if we stick with the marriage in spite of the conflict, we nevertheless avoid the issues of disharmony at all costs — swallowing our pride, sacrificing our values, forgoing our aspirations, and betraying our principles. We shut up in order to "keep the peace" — but it is not a genuine peace. It is only an uneasy truce which actually adds to the tension.

Whatever the nature of our problem, when we attempt to cope with it by ignoring it we succeed only in avoiding the expression of our humanity. Of course, there can be exceptions to this rule: there is no point in confronting hopeless odds. It is best not to disturb sleeping dogs — and certainly not napping gorillas. In general, however, it is not wise to avoid conflict. Only the appearance of conflict is dodged in this way; the true conflict travels with us, no matter how hard we try to escape it. At an appropriate time in the future, it reappears in a new format — in our next job, in a different city, with other neighbors, or with a different spouse.

Some people, unfortunately, cultivate the practice of avoidance in ridiculous extremes: they try to avoid almost *everything* in life, the pleasant as well as the unpleasant. They create a fantasy world which lets them tune out the happenings of daily life. Or they withdraw into a passive, catatonic state of indifference, induced either by their own fears, the use of drugs, or the practice of certain pseudo-meditative techniques. Some oriental gurus actually teach the avoidance of conflict as a way to cope with stress; they instruct their students to freeze their feelings and become emotionally numb. The result is a state of superficial niceness totally lacking in substance. These gurus talk glibly about peace, but achieve only a goofy state of blandness.

Other people practice the direct opposite of avoidance: they attack the sources of conflict viciously and almost dare stress to trouble them. These are usually people who dislike change of any kind and fight bitterly to preserve the status quo. They do not want to be forced to grow and become mature, and will use the psychological equivalent of guerrilla warfare to prevent it. Mothers who refuse to let their children grow up are an example of this attitude; they demean their kids, embarrass them, and force them into a groveling, dependent state that will carry on into their adulthood. In this way, they "eliminate" the stress of losing control of their children, but at the price of incurring the hatred, resentment, and rebellion of the offspring. It is not a profitable exchange. Moreover, the people who rely on this kind of tactic quickly become selfish, callous, and indifferent to the needs of others.

A second common but ineffective formula of dealing with stress is enchantment, in which we charm or seduce others into carrying our burdens for us. This trick is usually accomplished by appealing to the vanity of others, telling them they are so much stronger, or more talented, or better equipped than we to take care of the problem. Or their help is exacted as the price they must pay for our friendship or the romantic favors we dole out in return. This use of charm may serve to remove the immediate problem, but in no way does it help us become a stronger or more peaceful person. The people who do our work for us may learn these lessons, of course, but we remain weak, unskilled, and unable to handle stress. All we have is our charm.

Some people get others to handle their stress by acting as though they were totally helpless. Much illness is prolonged and aggravated by just this kind of an attitude. The illness becomes an excuse to force others to act on their behalf. The universe does not long indulge such behavior, however. Most people who try it soon find themselves abandoned, friendless, and uncared for. As a result, their stress is worse than ever.

As a last resort, very weak people will often try to handle stress by simply surrendering to it, allowing themselves to be swept away in chaos. They develop an enormous martyr complex, proudly stating: "This is just my cross to bear. It's too much, but I guess I'll have to suffer and endure. God must really love me to make me so miserable." In this way, they foster the illusion that there is virtue in suffering for suffering's sake. In extreme cases, these people either commit suicide as the "ultimate" form of avoidance or attempt suicide with the intent of failing, as a means of demanding that others help them out.

In society, whole groups of people sometimes use this method to cope with stress, by becoming professional "victims" of society and surviving on welfare or the guilt feelings of the stronger segments of society. It is a shortsighted solution, however, because the rest of society soon becomes irritated with them and cuts them off.

If we are genuinely dedicated to learning to handle conflict and stress to our advantage, we must eschew such magical sleights of hand, for only the nearsighted can be fooled by them. We must realize that no means of disarming turmoil will be satisfactory unless it leads to peace of mind and emotional peace, as well as to physical conditions of peace. If we fear reprisals for what we have done, or worry about losing what we have gained, or become ill in order to find temporary relief, then obviously we have not discovered peace at all. Consequently, we must carefully study the ingredients of peace known to our soul and duplicate them as best we can in our own attitudes and behavior. Fortunately, there are a number of practical steps which can be followed in generating the correct attitude of peace.

The first step is to cultivate greater *detachment* in the way we view distressful conditions. Detachment is the process of withdrawing our attention from the painful aspects of stress, refocusing it on our essential health and capacity to be a strong person who is able to achieve worthwhile goals. Just as we would not continue to hold our hand in a flame, letting it burn, once we had felt the heat, neither should we continue to hold our thought "fingers" in the midst of a painful problem, letting them suffer, once we have perceived the nature of it. It is much healthier to withdraw them and use our intelligence to correct the difficulty as best we can. This is the essence of detachment. In no way should it be confused with the state of indifference, however. The detached individual is able to comprehend the pluses and minuses of conflict objectively, and act accordingly. With detachment, we are able to recognize imperfection and be concerned enough to act to correct it, but we do not react emotionally, with hysteria or panic, to the unpleasant elements involved. Instead of falling into a fit of despair because life is imperfect, we choose to view the problem at hand as an opportunity to learn, to grow, and to exercise our skill and mastery.

Once a certain measure of detachment is achieved, it is then possible to identify with our innermost powers, strengths, and human qualities, by centering our life in our spirit. As we have seen, peace is found at the center of action—the center of stability, direction, and purpose. And so, if we can identify with the true source of our power and will, we will be greatly helped in coping with stress. We must be careful in how we proceed, however, for it is all too easy to identify with a "false center" which will not produce peace.

Some people know the value of withdrawing within themselves and finding their center of strength, stability, and peace, but they do not know where to look for it. So they crawl into a cozy nook of their subconscious, where they can create a fantasy world of peace and tranquillity, and believe they have found the center of their being. In actual fact, they have found only the heart of their wish life. They have centered themselves in their emotions—the most instable, capricious, and powerless portion of their humanity. An emotion is merely a sensation—not the source of consciousness nor a source of power.

There are many kinds of false centers in the emotions. Some people center themselves in the playful child they have always longed to be once again. Instead of seeking the maturity of the soul, they deliberately center themselves in greater immaturity. Others center themselves in their angry self-righteousness, becoming fanatics and bigots. But none of these false centers can ever become a permanent center of action or peace, because they all are located on the periphery of the personality. They are just artificial retreats. To have any value, the process of centering must focus us in the true source of our identity, our powers, our capacities, and our ideals—not just our feelings. We must become God-centered.

Once we do, it becomes possible to apply these inner strengths and qualities of peace in a most dynamic way. Before starting any project or undertaking which might involve stress, we can take a short amount of time to focus on the capacity of our inner being to deal with this situation efficiently and calmly. If we are familiar with an effective form of meditation, we can use that state of mind to identify with this inner formula; if not, we can merely reflect on and think about this dynamic contact being made. We rest a brief moment in the peacefulness of being aware that our highest self knows how to work successfully in this situation and will guide us as we proceed. This whole process of identifying with our inner peace, wisdom, and strength can be completed in just a couple of minutes. Then, if at any time during our activity we begin to perceive stress building up, we reinforce our inner peace by taking a few seconds—even in the midst of conflict—to quickly identify again with the inner pillar of wisdom which is the soul.

This practical formula can be applied to any type of activity—and should be, if we expect to nurture a beneficial contact with our inner source of peace. It should be used, for example, prior to difficult encounters with family members and tension-filled situations at work. It can also be used before pleasant but nonetheless demanding events. Even before playing a sport noted for the stress and tension it can produce—such as tennis or golf—we should take time to prepare to act peacefully.

The value of this simple technique, when mastered, cannot be overstated. And yet, it is not enough by itself. It helps us to develop the habit of turning our attention to the true center of peace within us—but once our attention is turned, we need to discover what it is we are looking at. Only then will the peace which resides within us come alive *for us*. This is best accomplished by taking inventory of our *assets in living*—our capacities to cope effectively with stress.

A good place to begin is by examining the personal resources and powers readily available to us for coping with difficult events. Knowing that the inner being has infinite resources of strength, wisdom, and power close at hand is of little use to us if we do not know how to convert them into endurance, good ideas, and effective action in moments of crisis. After all, having a million dollars in the bank is not much help if we are trying to park and do not have a nickel to put in the meter. So it is wise to take inventory of the practical skills, strengths, and qualities which already exist *within our personality*—and how we can use them to cope with stress.

If we have cultivated the ability to make effective decisions, for instance, then we should be able to handle an executive-level job without incurring excessive stress. If we have mastered the skill of inspiring other people to work effectively and productively, we should be prepared to fulfill managerial duties without unusual conflict. If we have learned the basic lesson of accepting criticism gracefully, we should be able to prosper in situations which put us in the public spotlight. If we are kind, considerate, and loving by nature, and able to accept responsibilities and fulfill them, we should be able to contribute to a meaningful marriage and family without expecting too much turmoil. Where we do not have these kinds of skills or talents in our personal inventory, however, we should diligently work to acquire them—or defer entering into situations where they are needed. Otherwise, we are inviting the natural stress which always attends incompetence or incompatibility.

Making the same kind of inventory on a group or national level can be useful in establishing peacefulness there, too. If we as citizens, for example, are willing to fulfill voluntarily the responsibilities of citizenship, then we should be well prepared to respect, honor, and properly apply freedoms and rights. If not, we are invoking inevitable conflict by demanding rights we cannot justify. Similarly, if we are generally well-educated, we should be able to understand the issues of government well enough to handle democratic representation. If not, it is likely that such a form of government will fail, shattering our peace.

It is also helpful to look at other assets on the personality level that we can rely on to cope with stress. An aspiring actor with good contacts in Hollywood, for example, will experience much less disappointment in starting his career than an unknown hopeful. A couple who share common interests, compatible ideas, and similar goals will experience less strife in establishing a peaceful marriage than a couple with nothing in common except a shared sexual interest. A political candidate with widespread popularity will have less difficulty in winning elections than someone who is generally disliked.

Proper attitudes toward life are also significant assets. As a general rule, the more we have unselfishly invested ourself in life, the more assistance we receive from the universe in coping peacefully with stress. Thus, the more we drive politely and courteously, the more other drivers will treat us in like fashion, eliminating much of the irritation many drivers face. The more we respect and obey the laws of the land as a basic attitude toward life, the more the law-enforcement agencies of our community will be responsive to us when we are in trouble. The more we help people in distress, the more we will be fortuitously assisted when we need help. The more we defend the integrity and honor of others who merit it, the more we in turn will be defended against malice and slander from others. On the other hand, if we approach life with a chip on our shoulder, we can expect everyone who comes along to try to knock it off. Our stress and discomfort will increase proportionally.

This honest inventory of our psychological and personal assets should be extended to include an examination of our goals, purposes, commitment, adaptability, and degree of involvement as well. For example, how willing are we to take risks? If we enjoy taking risks, we can obviously do many things without stress which would almost destroy someone who is meek and nonadventurous. Similarly, how willing are we to make compromises in order to achieve our goals? If we are a rigid perfectionist who insists on having everything our way, we are asking for an incredible amount of turmoil in almost every department of life. But if we are flexible enough to incorporate the ideas of others into our own plans, we can learn to work with a fair degree of peace.

In addition, it is also beneficial to determine the real sphere of our influence and the true dimensions of our responsibilities. Many of us incur great conflict by not putting reasonable limits on our self-expectations—we figuratively (and sometimes literally) kill ourself trying single-handedly to do the whole work of the universe and then some. Parents are a classic example of this problem. Most erroneously assume that they have lots of power to change their children and mold them in their own image. Then, when the children grow up and exhibit negative traits—from discourtesy to rebellion to dishonesty to outright criminality—they blame themselves and wonder where they failed. In some cases, they have indeed failed, but in the majority of instances the children brought these traits with them into life. The bad habits may remain latent during early childhood, but eventually they come into full flower—in adolescence or early adulthood. For parents to assume guilt for the failings of their children after they become adults is unreasonable in most cases. They are overestimating the sphere of their influence and thus suffer great distress. The same problem often occurs in business and industry, where managers overestimate the scope of their influence in changing their subordinates.

On an international level, a nation can open itself up to great conflict by assuming that it has a larger responsibility than it actually does. This kind of attitude contributed in part, for example, to America's rather foolish involvement in the internal affairs of Vietnam. The result was greater conflict, not peace.

One final asset to consider is our willingness to grow. How much are we ready to learn from any given situation? If we are willing to learn from embarrassments or failures, after all, we will be able to tolerate far greater amounts of stress and conflict than someone who takes such developments as personal insults. In addition, if we are able to see that we are indeed growing as a result of involvement in a difficult relationship, or trying conditions at work, we will gradually be able to reshape our perspective. What we once saw only as difficulty slowly becomes redefined as opportunity. What we once saw only as stress slowly is revealed to be the foundation of personal triumph—*our* personal triumph.

Achieving peace is a proposition which sooner or later involves every part of our livingness—our attitudes toward ourself and others, our skills and talents, our accomplishments and friendships, our contact with our inner self, and much more. It is not just enough to find peace in the heaven worlds; we must also create peace on earth, by living peacefully. And living peacefully is a fulltime endeavor; it is not possible to experience genuine peace in one aspect of life while failing to express it in another. We cannot know peace within, for example, at the same time that we are at odds with our environment or with other human beings. By the same token, as we make peace with life and our fellow voyagers, we establish the conditions which enable us to generate peace within.

Coping with stress and building peace are, of course, cumulative efforts. We cannot expect to eliminate a lifetime of worry, frustration, suffering, and hysteria in a week or two. Any progress we make is an important step in the right direction and cause for encouragement and hope. With enough small steps, we eventually find ourself marching to the beat of our own destiny and purpose. Then we know peace.

THE CALL OF PEACE

To know peace, we must become a God-centered person. If the wisdom, love, and strength of God form the nucleus of all our activities in daily life, there can be no room left for adverse emotional reactions to stress and suffering. If we are in God and God is in us, individually and collectively, we surely have the power and poise to deal effectively with any hardship or crisis which comes to us. Moreover, we have a basis upon which to build, grow, transform, and expand. Our dynamic inner center of peace becomes activated; it radiates outward into our life, projecting our ideals and goodwill into our work, relationships, lifestyle, society, civilization, and the whole of humanity. Peace always begins within, but as we come to know it we must honor it and help establish it on earth.

We are called to be peacemakers. There has been no formal proclamation of this duty, but it has been issued nonetheless. Every time we experience a bit of conflict or stress in our life, we are being called by the universe to be a peacemaker. Every time we worry or perceive imperfection, we are being tapped. We are being reminded to focus ourself in the peace, the order, and the service of God, so we may correct, transform, and redeem that which is lacking.

We are called to establish peace within ourself, so we may be an effective example to others. As the song expresses it, "Let there be peace on earth, and let it begin with me."

We are called to impose order, stability, and tranquillity in all we do, so imperfection and chaos are removed.

We are called to engage in skillful activity, for only in this way can God's plans and ideals become manifest peacefully.

We are called to encourage others to become peaceful, too—not by giving in passively to the whims of others, but by mutually respecting the divine ideals of life.

We are called to advocate the cause of genuine peace within the nations of the world, by revealing and nurturing the inner life of spiritual values.

As we answer this call, we begin to work in greater harmony with the evolutionary thrust of life. We help life unfold in an orderly manner; we inspire others to welcome and appreciate change, not fear it. We become a blessed child of God, as the Christ said we would.

Truly, only children of God can be genuine peacemakers. Only those people who have learned to center themselves in the life of God have the vision and understanding to eliminate conflict and redeem imperfection. To be a peacemaker, we must be aflame with the divine spark which fires our mind and floods our heart with goodwill, driving us to do and say those things that fulfill our destiny and help us participate in the works of humanity and civilization.

A man of peace is able to say in the midst of murderous conflict and opposition, "Father, thou art in me and I in thee." The moment of crisis does not shatter His peace, it increases it—He discovers an even closer contact with the God within, and with His fellow human beings. Thus, a man of peace can say to all of us, "In me you may have peace. In the world, you have tribulation, but be of good cheer—I have overcome the world."

Knowing this kind of peace, we can go forth and heal. We can go forth and build tomorrow's world. We can go forth and make known unto the world that which has been made known unto us.

ENLIGHTENED SELF-DISCIPLINE

Without self-discipline, the successful expression of any skill or talent would be impossible. But *enlightened* self-discipline adds yet another dimension to our activities—the inspiration and life of our innermost being. In this drawing, the well-disciplined dancer becomes a suitable channel for the creative will of his higher self, which subtly overshadows him. The result is an exquisite performance of beauty and grace.

A METHOD OF LEARNING

Human consciousness has turned out to be a remarkable mechanism. After all these lengthy eons, God's original model continues to be manufactured for popular distribution. Throughout the years, of course, there have been changes in human form and function, just as the features and performance of an automobile improve from year to year. But such modifications do not alter the original purpose of either an automobile or the human being. Indeed, as long as they are properly implemented, they actually enhance the usefulness and efficiency of both the machine and the man.

Automotive engineers and designers are constantly tinkering with the various component parts of the automobile, trying to improve it so it may better fulfill its purpose: to provide a reliable and comfortable means of personal travel. When a legitimate improvement in appearance, efficiency, power, or safety is incorporated into new models, it is quickly acclaimed and becomes a permanent feature. On the other hand, when an advertised improvement does not genuinely enhance the basic intent of automobiles, it is usually rejected by the public. Occasionally, however, the process of change is more complex — as in the case of improvements in pollution control and safety.

In these instances, the interests of the manufacturers have not always agreed with the needs of the public. When the manufacturers have failed to be duly self-regulating, regulation has often been forced upon them, by watchdog consumer groups, government agencies, and legislation.

We human beings likewise tend to tinker with the component parts in our mechanism of consciousness, trying to improve upon the basic model in order to achieve more fulfillment and know more satisfaction in life. We seek the ideal formulae for using our emotions, expressing our spiritual and religious urges, employing the body productively, juggling our attitudes, focusing our attention, harnessing the tremendous power of the mind, and building competence. In our quest to make the right changes, we spawn uncountable schools of philosophy, systems of religion, new therapies, self-help fads, educational disciplines, and meditative techniques. Some of these systems help us improve our ability to use the original model provided by God; some do not. In our enthusiasm, we sometimes even create methods which actually work *against* the purpose and intent of God's original prototype, thereby causing more harm than benefit.

Our human interest in improving ourself and what we can do, individually and collectively, is to be encouraged. The great achievements in civilization, art, literature, philosophy, science, and the art of living have occurred only because we have been willing to improve our condition and become more expert in all we do. But enthusiasm for change is not sufficient by itself; we must take care not to plunge unintelligently and capriciously into new experiments in human living, hoping that proper intentions alone will carry us through. Instead, like a good automotive engineer, we must try to anticipate which experiments in living will be successful and which are likely to backfire. To do this, we must become familiar with the original design for humanity and learn to evaluate objectively the kind of attitudes and activities that add to this design — and which detract. Then, we must develop the determination to live in accordance with our fundamental design — even when an alternate course of behavior may be emotionally more tempting or appealing.

In other words, we must become self-regulating, just as automobile manufacturers must be self-regulating or face the wrath of the government and public. For if we fail to be self-regulating, we have no means of connecting ourself with our most fundamental goals. Undirected, we wander aimlessly through life. If we fail to develop an inner set of rules, we have no reason to heed external rules. Unprincipled, we are unable to take advantage of opportunities for growth — and run the risk of incurring the disapproval of friends and society. Our vehicle of consciousness falters and stalls, no matter how we tinker with it; eventually, it ceases to serve its intended function altogether.

The usual term for the mechanism of human self-regulation is "self-discipline." In spite of present inclinations to disparage self-discipline, it is still a tool which is valued and used by every serious journeyman in the art of living. Indeed, it is an indispensable factor in individual growth and the evolution of humanity as a whole, for it is through the use of enlightened self-discipline that we learn to become self-supporting, self-activating, and self-governing.

The function of self-discipline is deeply rooted. One of the key features of God's original model for mankind is an element of free will which allows us to learn by experience. With each lesson in the art of living we learn, we become more skillful in transmuting experience into wisdom. Human experiences, however, come in different shapes and sizes. While some are easily handled, others test us to the very limits of our endurance, wisdom, adaptability, and compassion. If we make the mistake of approaching the experiences of life without self-discipline, we run the risk of being overwhelmed and thrown into despair. Moreover, we virtually guarantee that we will *not* learn any new lessons from the experiences—we will not acquire new insights, skills, or character strengths.

The purpose of self-discipline is to prepare the personality—the mind, emotions, and physical body—to be responsive to greater sources of wisdom or guidance, the challenges of living, and opportunities for contributing creatively to civilization. A "greater source of wisdom or guidance" might be a teacher seeking to help his students—or the inner being seeking to use the personality as a channel for its power, intelligence, and goodwill. A "challenge of living" might be a test of skill in an athletic contest—or the experience of handling a crisis at work or home. "Opportunities for contributing creatively to civilization" could range from the way we raise our children to the work of an artist, writer, or scientist. But no matter what the activity, if the personality is unable to concentrate its efforts, focus its attention, specialize its talents, persist in fulfilling good intentions, guard against inactivity or interruption, and resist temptations, it will have little chance of achieving its goals. At best, the undisciplined personality stumbles chaotically through life. A properly disciplined personality, therefore, has a great advantage over its unregulated counterpart: it is primed for meaningful growth and constructive involvement in life.

Unfortunately, the idea of self-discipline has been misconstrued by many people to mean some kind of punishment or reprisal. As a result, these people are quite willing to believe that self-discipline inhibits growth and self-expression. In point of fact, however, the word "discipline" originally meant a "method of learning" – a method to be used by a disciple or student to achieve greater competence and understanding in his special field of skill – or in life as a whole. Even today, this original meaning is preserved in the use of the word "discipline" to describe the various branches of knowledge or study at a university.

For a college student to master any particular field of study, he must train his mind to separate fact from fiction, discern which facts are relevant, draw appropriate conclusions, and apply those conclusions in a meaningful way. Such training also develops self-discipline in the student – at least in that aspect of his life – because he could never pass beyond the stage of separating fact from fiction without a well-regulated mind.

Some people argue that self-discipline makes us too rigid and uptight. We become so structured, they say, that creativity and good ideas cannot get through into expression. Typically, these gainsayers of self-discipline encourage us simply to experience "the flow of life." As pretty as such advice sounds, it is nonetheless an attitude which reduces human experience to the lowest possible level and robs it of its significance. It suggests that there really is no difference between fact and fiction, between relevance and irrelevance, and between accomplishment and failure. Its underlying implication is that what we experience has no value except for the sensation it can give.

If we are truly interested in making meaningful improvements in the form and function of God's original model, we must recognize this antihuman attitude for what it is: an attempt to weaken our self-control and self-respect, so that we can be more easily manipulated by latter-day wolves in sheep's clothing. Self-discipline, it must be remembered, is our mechanism for self-regulation. Without it, we are easy prey for others who might seek to regulate us for their own selfish ends.

It is important to understand, therefore, that effective self-discipline is not achieved by punishing, restricting, or inhibiting ourself. Quite the contrary, it is attained by *educating* ourself, just as the college student must educate himself to master his branch of study. Specifically, effective self-discipline is acquired by training the mind to recognize it has choices to make in any situation it faces—and that these choices become the framework for self-regulation.

The choices available are far more numerous than many of us suspect. Even when it seems that we have no choice in determining the outcome of an event, we nonetheless do have choices to make which will determine how we *react* to that outcome. We can choose to behave nobly or cowardly; we can choose to act maturely or petulantly; we can choose either to lose all hope or increase our faith. And we always have the fundamental choice of cooperating as best we can with the underlying patterns of order which subtly govern life—or defying them.

The unregulated, undisciplined person reacts blindly to the nature of events. If an event is unpleasant, he reacts with unpleasantness of his own. He does not take time to evaluate his choices or their possible consequences—he merely responds with a "gut reaction." In stark contrast, the disciplined individual carefully considers the consequences of the various options open to him, then selects the one course of behavior, thought, or attitude which will best enable him to reach his goal. An undisciplined athlete who has just made a mistake in his play, for example, might release his frustration by punching an opponent—or a referee. The disciplined athlete, however, rejects such behavior as unsportsmanlike, and chooses to dissipate his frustration by concentrating all the more fully on the next play.

The same patterns are observable in the happy moments of life, too. An undisciplined actor who receives a major role and great adulation may well become vainglorious and lose sight of everything except his immediate triumph. The disciplined individual, though, will enjoy his success without letting it disturb his deeper values, commitments, and professionalism. He rises above the temptation to become absorbed in the hero worship which follows him, and continues to pursue his craft.

Discipline, therefore, depends on having a clear understanding of the goals we wish to reach—and a definite commitment to reaching them. Having defined our goals in humanistic terms, so we know they are worthwhile and will produce consequences which will benefit us in the long term, we do not let anything stand in our way of consummating them—be it an internal weakness, the difficulty of the task, opposition from others, or even partial success. Obviously, this sort of self-regulation is not something which emerges overnight—or because we reach a stage in life in which we need it. It is a habit that is built over many years, as we formulate ideals and goals, establish values and convictions, and experience the results of our choices. Discipline does not prevent us from making mistakes, but it does permit us *to learn from those mistakes* and never make them again. The disciplined person reviews the results of his experiments in living and incorporates the lessons learned into his general outlook—which becomes the basis for subsequent decisions and actions. In this way, discipline grows and provides a valuable framework for our experiences.

The ability to make disciplined choices in life is extremely useful. It is the key to excellence in any endeavor—a point which is nicely supported by the examples of sports and the arts. Professional athletes do not just walk out on the field or court and start playing spontaneously. To reach the level of professional competition, they must spend hours and hours every day for many years practicing the different skills required by their sport. They must learn to endure physical injury and great discomfort, to suffer defeat, and to withstand great discouragement. There are countless times when they are tempted to abandon the hard work entailed in their sport and live an average life. But the choices they have made provide them with sufficient discipline to persevere. In making these choices, they are not restricting or inhibiting themselves; quite the opposite, they are preparing themselves for a much greater expression of their special talent than would otherwise be possible.

Discipline often involves the choice of many people to work together. A ballet troupe, for example, does not just show up on stage and perform. Its members have worked hard learning to interact smoothly with each other. The performance itself has been carefully choreographed, and the dancers have rehearsed it to the point of mastery. This choreography is part of their discipline—they are not at liberty to suddenly depart from the rehearsed plan and "do their own thing." Such undisciplined behavior would reduce the whole effort to chaos.

On the personal level, it is also discipline which keeps us from sliding ungracefully into the depths of confusion. At times we are all faced with ambivalence, having good intentions on the one hand but overpowering temptations and immature impulses on the other. Even an advanced individual such as Paul experienced this conflict, saying: "The good I would do, I do not, and the evil I would not do, I do." Paul knew the absolute necessity of discipline in coping with such ambivalence. He goes on to state: "I delight in the law of God, in my inmost self, but I see in my members another law." The urges of the body and the desires of the emotions can only be controlled, Paul was saying, by the disciplined choice to pursue the course of the inmost self. Indeed, it is self-discipline which enables us to *remember* our inmost self at these difficult moments, and give it the authority to stir up the good side of our personality and express it, while at the same time restraining our self-indulgent tendencies. Such self-restraint is neither inhibitive nor repressive; its function is to clear out the clutter of the personality and make it responsive to our inner goodness.

The undisciplined life has only marginal value—and worse, it is a pitiful state to experience. The undisciplined person wanders about in a fog of confusion, filled with false expectations. His inefficiency and incompetence draw the ire of those he must work with; he misses opportunities and good fortune, because he does not appreciate the way the universe operates. The noblest elements within him are forever being obscured by his lusts, cravings, and petty emotions. The selfishness of always wanting to have it his way, without discipline, gradually leads to an emptiness of spirit.

Most damaging of all, the undisciplined person is usually an individual who has long since lost his self-respect. He no longer has the ability to love his personality—he does not care what happens to it. He makes no effort to nourish it, protect it, or help it become better. As a result, he becomes trapped inside a confining prison (his own personality), starving to death spiritually. It is a bleak life, and it becomes bleaker as the years pass, because the lack of discipline and the lack of respect for his own livingness aggravate each other, making the situation more and more hopeless.

What must be understood is that discipline is an indispensable ingredient of love. While it is certainly possible to love someone who is not disciplined, it is quite impossible to express love or know love if *we are undisciplined!* Love languishes where there is no order or structure; it is suffocated by chaos. Those who believe that discipline involves suppressing the personality are therefore missing the point. In actual fact, self-discipline gives us *our only means* to honor our intelligence, goodwill, and creativity properly. It gives us the option to appreciate our humanity and our individuality—in a way the undisciplined individual can never experience, as long as he or she remains undisciplined.

An undisciplined life is a personal tragedy, but it need not continue to be one. Once the undisciplined person wakes up, appalled by his lack of self-respect and ability to function, he can recover and repair the damage done. The road to recovery begins with the recognition that *all* elements of his personality must be regulated.

Physically, he must regulate the appetites, compulsive habits, and urges of the physical body—not because they are evil or nasty, which they are not, but because the human being is designed to control the body, not be controlled by it.

Emotionally, he must learn to control his whims, imagination, reactiveness, and prejudices. This control is not achieved by suppressing his feelings as sinful, but rather by making sure that the emotions he does express consistently reflect the noblest, most ethical elements in his being—the qualities of love, goodwill, compassion, peace, harmony, sacrifice, kindness, and joy.

Mentally, he must develop the mind and begin applying its intelligence and common sense to the pursuit of worthwhile goals in life. This is done by defining values and convictions, translating them into meaningful goals and plans, and building the skills and capacities needed to implement them in his daily activities.

As the personality takes these first steps on the road to recovery, we begin to understand more about its nature, capacities, and function. This by itself is a major accomplishment, yet there is an even greater one to be attained: the ability of the well-disciplined personality to contribute to the work of the inner self. The inner being wishes to use its personality for enlightened self-expression, but where there is a lack of discipline in body, mind, or emotions, the intention of the higher self is thwarted. The life of this innermost part of our individuality is so well ordered and focused that it cannot express itself through chaotic or slovenly habits, careless attitudes, rebelliousness, or immaturity. A mental household which has been put in order, however, can be most useful to the inner self.

Indeed, to understand fully the significance of discipline, we must realize it is this innermost self which has the most interest in disciplining the personality. As we begin to see how the lack of discipline keeps us from being united with the best parts of our own being, we come to appreciate the full value of discipline. It is not just a method to train the personality for its own satisfaction; it is also a means of preparing the personality to be a skillful channel for the power, the intelligence, and the love of the soul.

Thus, we must strive not just for self-discipline but more importantly *enlightened* self-discipline—a program of self-discipline which will train the personality to be progressively more responsive to the soul. We must start with the basic assumption that the inner being is the proper authority for making changes in our life, our attitudes, and our behavior, and must base all of our choices on this assumption.

As we do, we begin to learn through direct experience that human consciousness really *is* a most remarkable mechanism, capable of wonders far beyond the average person's imagination.

THE WISE PARENT

One of the most persistent stumbling blocks for people who have sincerely devoted themselves to improving their personalities is the lack of discipline. They launch themselves on an impressive effort to change their habits, redirect their emotions, and train the mind. But once their initial enthusiasm wanes, they do not have the self-discipline to keep on working: to strive patiently, day by day, to effect the desired improvements. Instead of developing the mind to perceive the options of life, they allow themselves to be hypnotized by illusion, enchantment, self-indulgence, and sentimentality. As a result, they spend more time justifying the imperfections in their character than honestly striving to alter them.

In approaching self-discipline, therefore, we must be careful not to be distracted by sentiment and foolishly adopt a model for the disciplined life which would actually work *against* self-regulation and the authority of the soul. If we substitute illusion for clear thinking, we will be dooming our efforts to at least partial failure.

One false model of self-discipline championed by some is that of the Nazi drill sergeant who methodically stamps out any rebelliousness, bad habit, or fun. Such people harshly subject their personalities to strict deprivation; they often do succeed in becoming efficient in a machine-like way, but at the cost of destroying most of their human qualities along with the undesirable traits. Such pseudo-discipline stifles genuine learning, instead of encouraging it.

Other people quite correctly realize that discipline is a means of preparing the personality to be used by their innermost being, but then generate a false model by believing they must surrender themselves to the "will of God." The "will of God" may be embodied for them in a particular guru, or a Bible-banging preacher, or the emotional goo of their own subconscious impulses—but it is most assuredly *not* anything associated with God Himself. It is not and never has been the will of God for any human being to surrender to Him, becoming passive or submissive. Quite the contrary, we have been designed to *cooperate* with God as a full partner in His work. This noble destiny cannot be fulfilled as long as we are rolling around on the ground, or wallowing in emotional hysteria, or letting some other person (be it guru or a minister) amputate our capacity for free will. One particular guru from India, for example, speaks quite glibly about surrendering to the will of God, but his real motive is to recruit followers who will surrender to *him*. He has collected a large entourage of spiritually-castrated sycophants who have indeed suppressed some of their personal impulses. But this is not self-discipline—it is brainwashing. This so-called saint has created a walking mob of eunuchs, not enlightened disciples.

The act of *surrendering* to the will of God actually *suspends* our capacity to grow, because it is a denial of our own God-given ability to make intelligent decisions, to express love, and to live a competent, constructive life. Thus, it is the antithesis of enlightened self-discipline. To properly cooperate with God's plans and will, we must be able to discern, through a well-trained mind, exactly what His will and plan are. Then we must consider the various ways in which we, individually, can express them in our life. By acting in accordance with these intelligent perceptions, we automatically obey the will of God—but with wisdom, nobility, and dignity. Far from surrendering, we have triumphed as a human being.

Some people are attracted to the false model of surrendering to God as a way of disguising the fact that they have given up trying to cope with life. Overwhelmed by anguish and a troubled conscience, they abdicate their responsibility as human beings and childishly demand that God take over and run their lives. In this way, they attempt to blame God for their problems and failures, absolving themselves. As such, it is hardly a legitimate variety of self-discipline. In truth, there is no discipline to it at all—these individuals are surrendering to their own emotional chaos, not to God. Far from turning to the orderly and structured mind as a means of coping intelligently with pain or grief, they retreat into an undemanding state which comforts them but does not improve the quality of their life.

Of all the false models for self-discipline, however, perhaps the most disastrous is the belief that the spiritual person should be like a little child. Beset by the adult problems of discouragement, criticism, grudges, competition, anxiety, and fear, many people long fondly for a return to the comfortable times of their childhood. They observe that many children are quite peaceful and happy, eager to find out the way things work, incapable of holding grudges for any length of time, spontaneous and fresh, trusting, flexible and adaptable, and basically affectionate. They look at themselves and see many of these qualities missing, and decide the best way to discipline themselves is to become like a child. In doing so, however, they are not carefully observing the actual conditions of the child state; they end up longing for something which has never really existed. After all, children are happy and peaceful most of the time only because they are pampered and cared for by adults. The moment the pampering stops, most children begin whining. They have not yet acquired the maturity and discipline to realize that genuine happiness lies in self-sufficiency and competence. As for not holding grudges, it is only because children have not yet developed the kind of attention span needed to perpetuate them. Becoming like a child, therefore, will not eliminate the capacity to carry grudges—unless we simultaneously destroy our attention span. Fortunately, there are healthier ways to overcome grudges—by seeing, for example, that we have other, more mature options open to us. This same lack of maturity also explains why some children seem magically immune from anxieties, fears, and conflicts. These children have not yet grown up and developed a moral sense of integrity. They are still relatively unaware of the differences between right and wrong; their conscience is still essentially unformed. Consequently, they do not have the means to experience great conflicts. Indeed, difficult problems are usually taken to their parents to be solved. Even the fabled spontaneity and flexibility of children are more liabilities than blessings—because their minds are untrained, they have not yet been able to stabilize their character and personality traits.

These statements are not made as an indictment of children; childhood is an important stage in the development of the human personality. We must love children and help them mature into wise adults. But we must never be fooled by forgetting that children are basically immature. To romanticize the state of childhood and hold it up as a spiritual ideal is the height of silliness, and fundamentally regressive. It makes discipline impossible.

Indeed, it is the child within us which rebels against discipline, just as most physical children go through stages of rebelling against the authority of their parents. Children can be amazingly loyal to their parents as long as they are getting their own way, but as they become adolescents and learn about inner conflict and adult responsibilities, they classically reject their parents and all they stand for. This rejection is actually a rebellion against order and the need for maturity. The same pattern holds true for our growth as a human being. Even after we respond to the call of the soul and are pledged to enlightened growth, the child within us—our immature habits, attitudes, and whims—rebels and tries to sabotage the whole effort. Unless we are properly disciplined, this child within is often quite successful in interrupting our better efforts.

Sadly, some so-called spiritual teachers glorify the state of childhood and encourage their followers to mimic immaturity. Instead of talking about discipline, they talk about "playing." Their classes are without structure; they are quite content to let things happen spontaneously. The more chaotic a session becomes, the more they delight in it; like small children, they seem to enjoy loud noises, distractions, and disturbances. They thrive on excitement, not enlightenment. As a result, their teaching becomes the spiritual equivalent of disco dancing or rock and roll—thrills which satisfy only the lowest elements within us, completely obscuring our truly noble qualities.

Plainly put, childishness is not a reasonable model for the disciplined life. When a person tries to return to a childlike state, it is an open invitation for greater immaturity in his character, personal habits, and perspectives. He enters a fantasized state which is not just childlike but actually infantile; the child within his subconscious takes over. At times it is a playful, happy child, and it is easy to believe great changes have occurred. But just as often it is an irresponsible child, a child who wants to be pampered, a child who wants to be the center of everyone's attention, a very selfish child. The one child does not exist without the other. And so, becoming childish or childlike in our attitudes and behavior is a very regressive step, even though it sometimes seems to produce improvements. It is regressive because it sabotages all of our efforts to discipline the personality—and to become mature and competent.

Actually, the ideal model for self-discipline is just the opposite of the child within us. Enlightened self-discipline is best achieved by imitating the example of a wise, loving parent. A wise parent knows that a child—whether it is a physical child or the child within—needs to cultivate a good sense of discipline and order, if it is to mature. The wise parent values competence, responsibility, noble actions, and creative intelligence. And he loves and respects the child so much that he will take the time and energy to make sure the child learns the proper lessons. Even though it is often easier for a parent to indulge a child's whims than to be firm and insist that the child establish meaningful priorities, the wise and loving parent understands the danger of pampering the child. He chooses discipline instead.

At times the wise parent must restrict the activities or attitudes of the immature child. It may even be necessary to punish the child physically to convey the needed message. But the loving parent does not treat the child harshly or severely, even in these instances. He exercises firmness, yes, but does not condemn the child for being a child. Just so, as we pursue self-discipline, there will be times when we must restrict our own activities or attitudes. We may even have to restrain ourself forcefully at times, in order to conquer physical habits such as smoking or overeating. But there is never any reason for developing an antagonistic attitude toward ourself—despising our weaknesses or condemning ourself for alleged sinfulness. Instead, we should strive to be a wise parent who is capable of nurturing the child within us—the imperfect elements of our personality—while teaching it to behave in more adult ways. Thus, we stand firm and determined to improve our ways, never indulging our emotions or whims, but treating ourself with respect and kindness. After all, we deserve it.

The wise parent, of course, is a symbol for our own inner being, the soul. The soul already acts with the wisdom and love a good parent expresses. And it cares for the personality in the same way a parent cares for his or her child—if the personality is making the effort to discipline itself and become an effective channel for the qualities, inspirations, and life of the higher self.

For those who wonder how to improve their contact with the soul, the answer should now be obvious. What the soul most seeks in its personality is a high level of self-control and the willingness to cooperate with its guidance, regulation, and authority. Nothing improves our contact with the soul more quickly than the practice of enlightened self-discipline—and the readiness to accept the responsibilities of spiritual adulthood.

Let us therefore strive to be adults and leave the child within us behind. As Paul said, "When I was a child, I spoke like a child, I thought like a child, I reasoned like a child; when I became a man, I gave up childish ways." It is through enlightened self-discipline that we give up childish ways.

THE DANGER OF "LETTING GO"

Self-discipline is a natural expression of the fundamental order of the universe. This order is expressed in other ways as well: in the instincts of animals, the growth patterns of plants, and the structure of a solar system. In each of these examples, order manifests automatically. By contrast, since human consciousness has been endowed with the element of free will, our expression of order depends in part upon making the decision to be self-disciplined. And yet, as true as this statement is, it is equally true that we cannot mock the universe, no matter how much we may insist on abusing the prerogative of free will. God's basic plan for life will be fulfilled, whether or not we consciously cooperate with it. As a result, unless we are psychotic or senile, we undoubtedly express self-discipline in some way or another — either by choice or by default.

Unfortunately, not all of our expressions of self-discipline are enlightened. Some people, for example, use it to punish themselves, because they think themselves to be wicked and sinister. Others use a form of self-discipline to preserve bad habits, protect their selfishness, and express the dark side of their subconscious. Such people are confused about what self-discipline ought to be. Like the Nazi drill sergeant, they try to regulate themselves too harshly, and end up damaging themselves in the process. Unthinkingly, they attempt to keep control of their lives through suppression, repression, inhibition, and defensiveness. Yet none of these distorted expressions of self-control is a legitimate part of self-discipline.

Suppression is the conscious effort to restrict some impulse or habit without regard to the implications, origins, or consequences of the action of suppression. When we *suppress* anger, for example, we do not necessarily eliminate it — we just stifle it in our subconscious, where it will continue to burble and boil, making things worse in the long run. In *disciplining* anger, by contrast, we make the deliberate effort to change our attitudes and perspectives toward life, so as not to express anger in the future. We channel them into healthier modes.

Repression is the unconscious act of forgetting something which annoys us. The subconscious often uses repression defensively to avoid what the personality does not like—for example, forgetting a dentist appointment because we did not really want to go. Repression, therefore, represents a tendency to escape from the requirements or responsibilities of life. It is actually an opposite of enlightened self-discipline, because self-discipline helps us to recognize and fulfill our requirements and responsibilities more maturely.

Inhibition is the failure to act—mentally, emotionally, or physically—due to a lack of courage (*not* a lack of understanding or ability). A student who is afraid to speak because he feels he will reveal his ignorance is *inhibited*. Conversely, a student who refrains from speaking because he has nothing relevant to say is *disciplined*. Because the end results of inhibition and self-discipline are often similar, the two are frequently confused for one another. But the motivation and internal impact of each are completely different. Inhibition is motivated by fear, whereas discipline is motivated by wisdom—and usually a good measure of courage as well. Inhibition intimidates the personality, while self-discipline merely restrains the personality from making a fool of itself. Inhibition is neurotic and immature; discipline is an ingredient in health and maturity.

Defensiveness is the process of making choices which will help us avoid some kind of supposed stress. It is fundamentally selfish in character and does not promote constructive growth or activity. In this way it, too, is an opposite of discipline, because discipline is designed to encourage growth, not impede it.

The choice to be suppressive, repressive, inhibited, or defensive is not usually made deliberately; these problems occur primarily when we fail to make proper choices of self-discipline—when we fail to examine who we are and how we wish to act. In such cases, the choice may be made for us by others: our parents, social pressure, role models, friends, authority figures, or intimidating enemies. Or it may be made unconsciously, by uncontrolled subconscious drives. Herein lies the greatest potential for distorting the mechanism of self-discipline, because the average person living an unexamined life quickly becomes a victim of his own fears, anxieties, anger, and resentment. This garbage is dumped without processing into the subconscious and unconscious, but represents *choices* (unintelligent as they are) dictating future behavior.

If we have been using distorted forms of discipline, we must be careful to reorient our efforts in an enlightened way. For instance, if we have abused the purpose of discipline by being overly inhibited, it does not serve an enlightened purpose suddenly to remove all inhibitions. If we do, we are likely to end up being careless, lazy, and stupid—instead of a better human being. Or, if we are shy and defensive, it is not a good idea to try to cure our problem by taking the type of assertiveness training in which we will be taught to be angry, boorish, arrogant, and aggressive. This would only be a further distortion of our mechanism of self-discipline.

Sadly, many people attempt to cope with persistent negativity—be it pessimism, paranoia, self-pity, or hostility—by attacking their self-discipline, instead of nurturing it. They try to eliminate the inhibitions and obsessions which they think block their enjoyment of life, by destroying them in anger and rage. Certainly the need to find relief from negativity and anguish is most real, but assaulting the self-disciplinary mechanism as a means of gaining this relief is profoundly self-destructive. It damages the order-preserving function of the mind, and likewise offends the ethical and spiritual elements of consciousness.

Nonetheless, in our modern age there are many people who gladly lend moral support to such self-destruction. These people consider duty and discipline as threats to human happiness, believing any form of self-restraint or mature behavior to be a nasty inhibition. They decry the attempt to train the mind and expand its usefulness as unspiritual.

Instead, these false prophets of spiritual liberation promote a subtle form of hedonism which urges us to be spontaneous, "unprogrammed," and "in touch with our feelings." In order to achieve this state, they advocate "letting go" our inhibitions, "hang-ups," and restraints. But letting go is a very poor way to achieve maturity. It assumes that dumping out the bad automatically leaves the good. Actually, in most cases it leaves only emptiness. While humanitarian qualities do exist as a natural part of our inner being, they do not exist spontaneously in the human personality. Our character becomes kind, wise, loving, joyful, dignified, gentle, and forgiving *only if we make it this way!* Therefore, a person who lets go of his blocks and self-restraints, without simultaneously developing more enlightened qualities, becomes as "liberated" as an empty house whose doors and windows have been removed so that the wind blows through it freely! There is no good reason why anyone would want a house in such a condition. Nor is there any good reason why an intelligent person would want to let go of his self-restraints. The unrestrained, "free" person is at the mercy of any stray impulse, good or bad, which arises from within or without his consciousness.

It is true that the ethically motivated, disciplined person will suffer occasionally; his conscience will hurt him from time to time. He will suffer from frustrating sacrifices, be disturbed by criticism, and grieve over failure—because he cares about what happens to him. He honors his spiritual values and respects his commitment to intelligent living, and is bothered when he cannot measure up to his highest expectations. In these ways, he "enforces" his disciplined choices. Such "suffering," however, is not a long-term problem for him, because he knows it serves a useful purpose. It permits him to be an effective agent for service, a genuine humanitarian who embodies his convictions and values in his self-expression. Because he is self-disciplined, he is able to harness his personality—not to crush or inhibit his humanity, but to be creative, loving, and productive in life.

Nevertheless, the number of therapists, educators, and gurus who consider such a person "hung-up" is legion. Empty-headed themselves, they encourage their clients, students, and followers to empty themselves as well, by acting out their negative impulses and by attacking every "repressive" thought or feeling. And yet, such destruction of the self-disciplinary mechanism is as foolish as smashing a fine wristwatch with a hammer, because the wheels and gears have become clogged with dirt.

To some, it may not seem that "letting go" our inhibitions or pressures could possibly harm the disciplinary system. But in the process of letting go, we become indifferent and cavalier. We pay less attention to our conscience. We begin to rationalize away our values, our goals, and the deepest signals of guidance within us, because they conflict with our efforts to "flow with the moment." As a result, the elements of consciousness which tend to integrate the personality and give it a clear definition begin to dissolve. If "letting go" is continued at that point, we soon end up bereft of the very qualities and attributes which make us human. We descend into chaos.

At the same time, we progressively retreat into our feelings or emotions. Indeed, most people *justify* "letting go" as a means of "getting in touch with their feelings." But this is not the marvelous step they believe it to be. Retreating from self-discipline into our emotions is an open invitation to self-deception. It is like surrounding ourself with a coterie of sycophantic friends who will shower us with praise, but never a helpful or critical word. The emotions delight in comfort, and if given free rein, will do what is necessary to attain or preserve that comfort. In most people, this means creating an elaborate fantasy world with little correspondence to reality. Tragically, the retreat into our feelings often ends in a life dominated by hysterical reactions and paranoid and fanatical obsessions.

By nature, discipline works through the mind, which is stable, and not the emotions, which are volatile. According to God's original model for the human being, it is the mind which is designed to perceive order and express it. It is the mind that is capable of comprehending the purpose of life and basing enlightened choices on it. Any retreat into our feelings jeopardizes self-discipline.

Only the mind has sufficient integrity to make the choices required for self-discipline. It may seem to some that the emotions can be used perfectly well to make choices—for example, what we like and dislike. But the emotions respond primarily to blind impulse and the "line of least resistance." The feeling that a genuine choice is being made is therefore completely illusory—it is nothing more than the kind of "choice" presented to the voters in a Soviet election.

Without the integrity the mind can provide, we may find it difficult to implement the disciplined choices we have made. If the emotions are unhappy with our choice, for example, they may put up quite a struggle. And so, if our intent to establish order in life and subdue chaos is serious, we must be willing to *restrain* the temptation to pursue the alternatives we have ruled out. Instead of attacking self-discipline as repressive, we must give full authority to the wisdom within us to regulate and restrain our wishes, desires, and fancies. Only then can our personality become fully expressive of the greatness within us.

Indeed, any attempt to circumvent the regulatory mechanism of human consciousness by taking a vacation from our duties and discipline *cheats* the personality by denying it rational direction—and separates it further from the power and purpose of the indwelling spirit. It does not matter what pretty phrases or popular "psychobabble" are used to make it sound better. Claiming to have "chosen" this course of action does not hide the fact that we are actually abandoning or even destroying our capacity to make choices! Nor does it do any good to pretend that "anything I want to believe in is real for me, and my reality is just as good as yours." A pretense is still a pretense, and will eventually generate increasing stress and strain in life.

Sometimes, the process of "letting go" is even given a vicious twist—we are encouraged to attack the supposed cause of our repressed feelings or inhibition. For example, we may be told to imagine ourself brutally "telling off" or defying the boss we do not get along with or the parent who taught us a bad habit when we were a child. Unfortunately, anger is a powerfully destructive force; far from improving the quality of our consciousness, any expression of hostility or vengeance endangers our self-regulatory mechanism. The whole fabric of our consciousness is weakened by it. If repeated often enough, anger can seriously jeopardize our capacity to control even automatic behavior—possibly to the point of senility.

Another great danger of "letting go" is that it can easily encourage an attitude of indifference toward rules and regulations. We begin to indulge every indiscriminate wish of the personality—on the assumption that it is more important to protect our feelings than it is to respect the values of other people and society. At best, this attack against self-discipline results in a very selfish person who tries to justify his selfishness by claiming that only the "now moment" is important and by professing to be "totally honest" with himself. At worst, it results in criminal attitudes toward life and a tendency to bully and manipulate everyone else. These people often do seem to have their feelings of guilt, fear, anger, remorse, discouragement, and indignation well disciplined, but in truth they have smugly and arrogantly squelched them. If the alternative to guilt is criminality, then surely guilt is the more preferable. But such people are too selfish to understand this—and too much blinded by their remorseless indifference to see that there *is* yet another choice.

Thus, while "letting go" may appeal greatly to some people, it must be clearly understood that what such people are letting go of is the very possibility of maturity. They are letting go of the key to human dignity, personal improvement, and self-respect. They are letting go of the opportunity to love and be loved. They are rejecting their highest impulses, and are instead genuflecting at the feet of a golden calf, worshipping the counterfeit idol of their own whims and wishes.

Once we begin to recognize the true nature of *enlightened* self-discipline, and can distinguish it from its distortions, it becomes possible to appreciate its significance more completely. Enlightened self-discipline conditions our personality to become responsive to the highest, wisest forces within us, and to embody this wisdom in desirable patterns of behavior. It reinforces good intentions, strengthens our motivation, starves out bad habits, and nourishes beneficial ones. It permits us to comprehend our identity and individuality more fully, while increasing our capacity to interact with others and participate in group activities.

In addition, enlightened self-discipline enables us to focus and apply the spiritual will in our personality. The spiritual will is the *power* of our inner life, the key to self-determination, inspired leadership, and the higher expressions of creativity. It can only be contacted by highly disciplined people. Emotional zombies who have "let go" of themselves or surrendered to the supposed will of God are light years away from the spiritual will. But the individual who is willing to practice self-control soon learns to handle more than just himself, and thereby sets the stage for acquiring transcendent skills in living. It is then that the spiritual will begins to act in his life, attitudes, and plans.

And the child inherits the wisdom of his parent.

A HABIT OF ACTION

Enlightened self-discipline is a noble activity which calls forth the highest elements within us. It honors these elements and puts them to work, creating a better self-expression. Any effort to develop enlightened self-discipline, therefore, will be most successful if we start from a point of poise. A poised attitude links us with the noblest qualities within us. By contrast, the frenetic emotions and hysteria usually accompanying the process of "letting go" link us with bewilderment. Order cannot manifest itself as long as we are indulging in chaos and confusion. And so, we must calm down and still the emotions, so the mind can be more easily guided by its wisdom. It is not especially hard to achieve this calmness; there have been many times in life when we have been relatively poised. By recalling them, we can reestablish an effective measure of self-control.

Many fears, inabilities, and other undisciplined parts of life remain difficult to control primarily because we panic whenever exposed to them. If we fear heights, for example, we become so hysterical when near the top of a tall building that our self-disciplinary mechanism becomes inoperative. If we take time to calm down and regain our poise *before* going to the top of the building, however, our mind (which is not afraid of heights) will have a better chance of keeping the emotions (which are) in line.

Having established a degree of poise, we must then recognize the capacity of our inner being to guide us in making the changes we seek. It is always the personality which must initiate and persevere in the process of self-discipline. But it is the power and guidance of our inmost self that will be our real strength in difficult moments of stress and temptation. We may not be able to imagine our personality having the courage to conquer our fear of heights, for example, but it is easy to realize that the inner self does. How could the soul — an infinite fount of poise and strength — possibly be afraid of anything? Thus, we must acknowledge the full authority of the parent within us to instruct the child within us in new directions—and to enforce this instruction as necessary. By tapping into its strength, we, too, share in that strength, and gradually learn to express it through our personality.

The strength of the inner self or soul does not flow into the personality just because we would like it to, however. We can only tap into it by carefully and patiently developing an adequate channel in our livingness through which it can act. This channel is created by properly training the mind. Only the mind is suitable for this work. The emotions are too instable to maintain a channel, and the body is too concrete.

Our greatest effort in becoming more self-disciplined, therefore, must be to activate the mind. This is an ongoing proposition requiring years to achieve fully; it is not enough just to spend a few minutes a week thinking about the issues of discipline. We must virtually *feast* at the banquet table of the mind, stuffing our hungry curiosity and need to know with all sorts of ideas, perceptions, conclusions, and realizations.

To whet the appetite, we must learn of our potential for self-determination. While much is made in our modern society of the need for self-*expression,* it ought to be remembered that human expression is often silly and pointless. It only becomes purposeful as we learn self-*determination*—as we learn to focus our free will intelligently and put it to work in service to creative goals and ideals. We must lift our sights from the trivial elements of life which preoccupy so many people and clearly define just what is possible—and practical—for us to do. In this way, we prepare ourself to make the choices and decisions which become the fabric of self-discipline.

The key to becoming self-determining is to think

through and evaluate our values, ethics, and convictions as they apply to every aspect of life. What are our moral principles? Are they based on the ideals of the inner self and the nature and laws of the universe? Or have they been formulated by default, in reaction to the programming of others or a limited set of experiences? Do they help us aspire to transcendent elements of life, or drag us down into compromise, expediency, and selfishness? How well do we honor these values, ethics, and convictions in our daily acts, attitudes, and feelings?

The work of discerning and defining our values and ideals requires the meticulous use of the mind. There is a great temptation to acquire values and ideals *by assumption,* without spending time contemplating them or understanding them. We assume certain values or ethics are useful to us—because others embrace them, too, or because they appeal to us emotionally—but we never really integrate them into our attitudes or behavior. The assumption of values certainly requires less work than the process of intelligent examination and soul-searching, but it produces only a superficial interaction with ideals. It does not help us become self-determining; it does not strengthen our capacity for self-discipline.

It is important, therefore, to build an intelligent core of values and principles of our own, based on our observation, evaluations, reflections, and conclusions. Properly constructed, this central core of ideals will become the foundation upon which the whole of our thinking will be created—the backbone of our self-discipline.

From these values and convictions, we must next shape meaningful goals. By its very nature, the act of setting goals imposes order on life. It likewise activates our self-determination, for as we focus the mind by considering the goals we wish to reach, we magnetically draw to us the conditions which will help us achieve them. In setting goals, however, we must take care to examine their implications. What will be the consequences of attaining these goals? Is the price we must pay worth the gain we anticipate? Will these goals further the enlightened purposes of our innermost self?

In order to answer these questions, we will have to ponder the way the universe itself behaves — its laws of right human relationships, cause and effect, economy, and purposeful action. This work, in turn, will give us a basis for ordering our priorities and developing specific plans — plans both for initiating constructive action and for seizing opportunities which arise.

Up to this point, the focus of our effort has been to formulate goals, plans, and convictions about how the *personality* should live. But it is also important to seek the greater perspective of the *soul,* at its own level. In doing this, we must be careful not to be distracted by long-standing weaknesses, glamours, illusions, self-deceptions, blind spots, or wishes of the personality. Too much attention to any of these aspects of the "child within" can jeopardize our integrity. Therefore, we should always keep in mind that we are seeking to contact the power of the spiritual impulse and purpose within us — not the power of our emotions. This spiritual power is tapped by learning to perceive and act upon the meaning and value of every element of life.

In this regard, it will also prove helpful to learn to recognize when the soul approves of the actions of the personality. Lacking this ability, we cannot properly grow from our experiences. The principal sign used by the soul to convey its satisfaction is a subtle joy of fulfillment which fills the active mind. It can easily be missed by people who are accustomed to the uncontrolled ecstasy of the emotions, but nonetheless is an important signpost to recognize.

As these skills develop, it also becomes possible to activate the will aspect of consciousness. This, too, is a vital step in nurturing self-discipline. However, we should be careful not to confuse the will with mere stubbornness or inflexibility. Stubbornness and inflexibility are outgrowths of strong, selfish emotions. The will, on the other hand, is the *urge to do,* the impulse to make something manifest, to achieve a certain goal, or to create something worthwhile. It is the essence of power, and exists independently of intelligence and feelings.

The will is often thought of as very mysterious, but it can actually be activated in simple and practical ways. The key is realizing that we have the capacity to choose the impulses and urges which will be our primary sources of motivation. Instead of being driven by the grossest urges within us, as any animal would be, we have the opportunity to choose to respond to humanitarian impulses and noble urges—for example, the intention to promote civilization, honor brotherhood, and serve God. By refining the urges and drives within us, so they become responsive to our values and ethics, we tap the power of will.

As we learn to use the will, we must remember that the suppression of urges and impulses is *not* a part of enlightened self-discipline. Neither is it a valid use of the will. Instead, the will is designed to be used in harnessing the forces of the personality for constructive activity, just as the power of Niagara is harnessed to generate electricity without marring the beauty of the falls itself. A classic example of harnessing the forces of the personality is the artist who sublimates his sexual drive and applies this force to his creative productivity. The artist does not impair his sexuality by sublimating it; he simply learns to focus a great energy and find additional enlightened uses for it.

The will is developed by learning to recognize, accept, and use the power of meaningful purpose, which underlies all of life. The person who does not see the meaning and purpose in what he does becomes absorbed in a sponge of triviality. But the individual who perceives purpose in the events of life, even the seemingly insignificant ones, has found a genuine key for cooperating with the order and laws of the universe. This recognition in turn releases a profound measure of the will. Ultimately, it is the will which ensures the success of discipline.

Even if we follow all these suggestions, however, there will be times in our efforts to increase discipline when we stagnate. We have built the mind to the point where we understand what we need to do, and why we should do it, and how great the benefits are. But we fail to do it. We have great poise and recognize the authority of the soul in our life. But we are unable to act. We even know how to direct the will at the resisting forces in the personality. But nothing budges. We are at a standstill.

In such instances, it is helpful to remember the love and respect the wise parent, the soul, has for the child, the personality. This child has a noble destiny and purpose, which must be honored. It is worthy of being loved, respected, and appreciated—not with self-indulgence, but as a mature act designed to remind the personality that self-discipline is not a horrible restriction. It is a step forward into enlightenment.

If done properly, this simple exercise helps us realize

that we love our personality so much we cannot bear to let it continue to be undisciplined any longer. We respect our intelligence so much it is no longer possible to succumb to bad habits, undignified urges, or irresponsible behavior. We value our destiny so much we can no longer afford to put if off by being lazy. Like the wise parent, we know the child sometimes has a mind of its own, but we also realize that we love it so much no sacrifice is too great to help it become perfect, even as our Father in heaven is perfect.

Without having prepared our mind and activated our will first, the realization of this love will not accomplish very much. Love complements but does not replace either intelligence or power. Only when we have learned to focus power, wisdom, and love *together* in our consciousness have we acquired all the tools we need for self-discipline.

Nevertheless, we have not completed the process of developing self-discipline. We still must learn to act responsibly in life, and not turn the power of discipline to unintelligent, selfish, or antihuman ends. We must come to understand that we are accountable for our actions, and start looking for and accepting the consequences of what we do and fail to do. Guided by our principles and ethics, we must amend our behavior in the light of these recognized consequences. Moreover, we must understand and accept the reality of the inner life, as well as the fact that many choices and plans affecting our discipline have already been made for us—by the soul. Indeed, the soul will be accountable and accept responsibility even if the personality does not! This inner accountability directly affects the quality of our life. If we try to defy it, the soul forces us to recognize its value and purpose. Since we probably will not enjoy the way the soul demonstrates this lesson to us, the disciplined choice is to act responsibly in life from the outset.

Above all, we must never degrade the potential of self-discipline, thinking of it only as an interesting philosophy, or a tantalizing subject to discuss over coffee and cookies. To be effective, self-discipline must become a *habit of action,* an integrated aspect of all we do. It does little good to train the mind to contact the authority of the inner self if we continue to indulge our laziness and slovenliness. It serves no real purpose to build talents and ideals if we continue to permit our emotional reactiveness and prejudices to make our most important decisions about using them. The process of discipline, therefore, is completed by seizing the opportunities which come to us to use our talents, ideals, and noble intentions to accomplish something meaningful. In some way, we must add our bit to the welfare of humanity, civilization, and the universe. Our contribution need not be spectacular, but it should embody the many facets of discipline which have been outlined here. It should express purpose, order, enlightened will, unselfish goodwill, ethical conduct, and a noble heart.

This is the goal of self-discipline.

LIBERATING THE SPIRIT

Fully developed, self-discipline is something like a water system for a large city. Because it is impractical for residents to collect rainwater in barrels, the city builds a system to gather the water from rivers or reservoirs, pipe it to central stations, purify it, and then pump it to the many homes, businesses, and public places it serves. The whole process of moving this water to the consumer is an organized one which must be carefully regulated. The water cannot be pumped through ditches, for example—that would breed disease. Nor can the purification process be erratic—it must be carefully planned and monitored. In a similar way, discipline serves the function of providing a channel through which the power, intelligence, and love of the inner being can flow into the personality—and furthermore, a means by which the personality can competently express those energies in daily life. To be undisciplined would be tantamount to waiting for a little rain to fall, trying to catch it in pots or pans. Or, for some people, it would mean trying to steal the water supply others have collected for themselves.

The disciplined energies of power, intelligence, and love can be focused into the personality for any number of uses. They can be used to change habit patterns, overcome laziness, develop patience, temper urges and cravings, and improve attitudes. They can be helpful in stimulating our will to learn, enabling us to benefit more fully from schooling, concentrated work, or meditative endeavor. And they can be put to work in any practical or creative activity: in sports, the arts, teaching, leadership, science, or any realm of valid achievement.

And yet, there is also a transcendent use of self-discipline. Enlightened self-discipline is an activity which truly helps to liberate our spirit in the midst of daily life. Only the disciplined, enlightened individual is genuinely free, in spite of all of the misleading claims of the people who preach "letting go." Enlightenment is a state of awareness achieved by building up in our personality the qualities and talents which allow us, *as a personality,* to serve the inner life. Then, as we serve the inner life in all that we are and all that we do, *by acting with enlightenment,* we transform our character. Once selfish, childish, and self-indulgent, we begin expressing the noblest elements within us.

It is at this point that we become aware consciously of the actual design of God's original model, the prototype human being. We marvel at it, because it *is* a remarkable mechanism. We appreciate how well it has served us in reaching this point, a point at which we become a suitable companion of the Creator and a proper steward of His creations. Then we truly can honor the inner life—within ourself and within the universe—and we can accept expanded responsibilities as citizens of the universe and children of God.

Through proper discipline, the personality can reach its highest function. The child matures and becomes an adult. And when it does, the wise parent within us is proud to say, so that we may hear: "This is my beloved Son, with whom I am well pleased."

INSPIRED HUMILITY

Reverence in Action

Far from abasing us and making us feel unworthy, as many suppose, inspired humility helps us become more aware of the noble and decent qualities within us. Humility is best expressed by standing upright, unafraid to meet our inner greatness face to face. Then we discover that our inmost essence is cut from cosmic fabric—a revelation worth humbling ourself before.

A ROBE WITHOUT ANY SEAMS

One of the great attributes which distinguishes mankind from the animal kingdom is the ability to stand *erect*. Instead of crawling on all fours, man is designed to walk with his head elevated to the heavens and his feet treading firmly on earth. As he walks, the movement of his feet is to be guided by signals from the head. In this way, ideally, man gradually learns to unite intangible heaven with tangible earth, spiritualizing and enriching it with new life. But this purpose cannot be served if we are unwilling, individually or collectively, to stand upright and express our human dignity.

Our posture toward life is of utmost importance. If we slouch through life, too lazy to make a greater effort, we develop a spiritual hunchback which hinders our aspiration. If we stumble stupidly through life, not taking the time to think carefully about our values and goals, we trip over obstacles and bruise our self-expression. But saddest of all, if we deliberately degrade our potential by feeling unworthy to walk and stand upright — by falling to our knees and crawling through life — we estrange ourself from the best within us, from our spiritual purpose, and from the treasures of heaven. We jeopardize our heritage and promise as a human being, becoming little more than a tired beast of burden, fit only to be used and abused by others.

Unfortunately, we are often encouraged to betray our capacity to stand erect, aspiring to heaven, and are instructed instead to cast our eyes downward. We are told to fear God and quake before the prospect that He will smite us down for our multitude of sins, real or imagined. We are taught that we are stained with evil and therefore unworthy of hope or consideration — unless we do as we are told and believe as we are told. Whole strata of society have been conditioned to feel inferior and not make any effort to improve themselves; others have been told the price of success and comfort should be a sense of guilt — that they are somehow personally responsible for the failure of large masses of humanity to acquire the same measure of competence, wealth, creativity, or goodwill as they. In communist countries, citizens are taught that only the state counts. Individual members of the state do not have any significance apart from the welfare of the commune or nation.

In many subtle ways, every day, we are reminded that if we have accomplished something worthwhile or developed a good idea, we had better not talk about it — at least not in honest terms — lest we *embarrass* others who have not distinguished themselves in any worthy way or *threaten* those who are ashamed of their incompetence. Pride, we are told, is a deadly sin — and it is blasphemy to believe that we, as human beings, can truly excel or become divine.

These degradations are taught us in the name of "humility." And, since we have been told that humility is a spiritual ideal, we accept what we have been taught. After all, the meek shall inherit the earth. But what do we truly know of humility?

For most of us, being humble means always keeping

our inadequacies, limitations, and imperfections uppermost in mind, never becoming too enchanted with the "dangerous" concept that we might possibly be competent or creative. It means denying the value of our good ideas, being ready to apologize for our achievements, and always being afraid to look at God directly, face to face. We may or may not embrace the wisdom of these canons of the humble life, but most of us do base our attitudes upon them. Not wanting to be accused of pride or self-importance, we dutifully grovel, like a savage participating in a pagan ritual, before the Altar of the Fallen Angel, denying our self-worth in an orgy of humiliation.

Sometimes the message of humility is impressed upon us subtly, as when we are chided for being pleased because we have successfully demonstrated a special talent or knowledge; at other times, it is blatantly pounded into our character, as when we are bombarded by the bombast of a priest or minister who gleefully informs us that we are contaminated by original sin, unworthy of God's love, and doomed to burn forever in hell, unless we repent. Of course, there are also times when the wounds of humiliation are self-inflicted.

For the intelligent, discerning person, however, the common practice of linking humility with the practices of self-abasement, unworthiness, and contrition is confusing and bewildering. How can it be healthy to debase the worth of our humanity—to deny our innate capacity to grow and become a better person, individually or collectively? Can it be a spiritual ideal to tear down anything—most of all the value of human consciousness? If the Christ encourages us to do all that He has done, *and even greater things,* then is any good served by pretending we cannot? Can we really stand upright so long as we are on our knees, groveling?

The answer is *no*. Linking humility with self-abasement, unworthiness, and contrition is an unholy alliance, antihuman and anti-God. It estranges us from our talents and widens the gulf between the personality and the soul, between humanity and the Father. It dwarfs our character and stunts our capacity to grow. It seals off doors of consciousness through which opportunities for service and new awareness might enter. We begin to expect that we will make mistakes, offend God, and be unable to achieve meaningful growth or success. Slowly, our capacity for self-respect atrophies, leading to a chronic state of pessimism and dissipation. Our enjoyment of life fades, overwhelmed by grimness and the burden of sin. The sphere of our life experiences contracts, until we truly feel less significant than a worm.

Surely we deserve better! Nothing is gained by humiliating ourself in these ways, either before the specter of a terrifying God, a government which denies our freedoms, or acquaintances who try to sabotage our dignity. Life is too noble to spend it cowering before the shrine of self-abasement. Therefore, instead of crawling on our knees, afraid to look upward, we should remember it is part of our original design as a human being to stand tall and strong—with nobility, self-possession, and courage. God made worms to crawl on the ground, but made humans to stand erect, physically, emotionally, mentally, and spiritually. Strength of character is nothing to be ashamed of—nor anything to apologize for.

In point of fact, the popular definitions of humility are gross and obscene distortions of the noble purpose of humility. In its inspired form, humility is an important ingredient in the art of living—it helps us establish our proper and just relationship with our inner being, other people, our nation, and God. It assists us in appreciating the good elements within us, thereby enabling us to enjoy the fruits of life more fully and develop our talents and abilities. It teaches us to respect life and revere God's noble purpose. *But it never belittles nor humiliates us.* True humility never forces us to our knees in a confession of inadequacy; it never crushes our spirit in pointless contrition. Far from diminishing our sense of self-worth, inspired humility *magnifies* the presence of life within us, so we may glorify it in all we do.

To understand this true nature of humility, it is helpful to know something of the psychology of enlightenment. Esoterically, it is held that the human personality has been created by the soul for the purpose of executing an important piece of work—namely, adding the light of spirit to the earth plane. Due to the dense nature of the earth plane, this spiritual light must be absorbed gradually. The human personality was therefore designed so it might *evolve,* from a relatively simple level to a much more complex one. As this evolution proceeds and each human being learns to operate in better and more enlightened ways, the whole of life around us becomes more enlightened as well. Each of us individually contributes to this process by recognizing our weaknesses and imperfections and working to correct them. All of us collectively contribute by recognizing the ills and errors of society, nation, and civilization, and working cooperatively to heal them.

The problem is that many of us *overrate* the role of the personality, ignoring the soul and its noble purpose. Humility, in its true form, is the spiritual quality which helps us remember the heritage of the soul and its purpose. It recognizes the distinction between the personality and the soul, and places these two aspects of our being in proper perspective. The humble person is one who acknowledges the authority of the soul and the noble nature of its destiny—listening for its guidance, consulting its wisdom, and accepting its plan for his life. He *respects* the presence of God within him. But in no way does this imply that he downplays the significance of the personality. The humble person knows the personality is the beloved creation of the soul and is meant to glorify the soul's love and wisdom through its daily thoughts, feelings, and behavior. Therefore, he respects not just the divine nature of the soul, but also the potential of the personality for enlightened self-expression. *This* is the proper use of humility.

The very word "humility" embodies this idea. Our modern English word derives from the Latin word *humus,* meaning "earth." Knowing this, it is easy to see why some people equate humility with the act of groveling in the dirt. But that is a degradation of humility. In its highest sense, humility is the act of relating the earth plane with the plane of spirit—in other words, relating the personality with the soul.

Humility is an affirmative act of respecting our own greatness and nobility as a human being. It is a recognition that we have a divine birthright, which we are fully entitled to express in our daily life. There is *nothing* negative nor destructive about humility. Only the counterfeit versions undermine our self-esteem and abase our dignity.

To some, this definition of inspired humility may sound more like pride—and, of course, we have been taught to condemn pride. But this, too, is a tragic error: there has been as much misunderstanding of pride as there has been of humility. In part, this confusion stems from the fact that the English word "pride" has lamentably been used to refer to two very different human attitudes. On the one hand, "pride" is often used to describe a state of being well-pleased with what we have accomplished—knowing we have done something useful for humanity, or something which satisfies the expectations of our inner being. On the other hand, "pride" is also used to refer to a state of being excessively conceited and arrogant—especially when what we have accomplished does not really merit our boasting and bragging. We are pretending we have done something worthwhile, but in truth we have not.

It would be best not to use the word "pride" to refer to this latter state of boasting and conceit, substituting the word "vanity" instead. At the very least, it should be called "false pride," and we should stop believing genuine pride to be something sinful and harmful. It is not. "Pride" is a noble word which rings with strength and courage; the act of taking pride in our legitimate achievements is an important part of maintaining our psychological health and balance. What we do in our life *is* important and significant, even on a cosmic level, *if* we recognize this importance and significance and instill it in our good works. To boast dishonestly about it is false pride—we are living a lie, which is always harmful to our well-being. But to conspicuously deny the significance of our contributions and our potential is false humility—and every bit as much a lie.

Genuine pride, therefore, nicely complements inspired humility, by giving the personality an opportunity to praise the soul for its assistance, and by giving the soul the chance to strengthen its bond with the personality. Far from being opposites of one another, as is commonly supposed, pride and humility are tools meant to be used *together,* as we strive toward enlightenment. They help us build our inner strength and thereby stand upright, able to walk forward into the full light of day. They help us transform the personality from a weak, submissive, vulnerable, and inherently selfish mass of confusion into a worthy channel for the expression of divine love and wisdom. Pride and humility, blended together, awaken us to a realization of who we are, what we can do, and the value of our life.

Indeed, the way in which we choose to express humility and pride reveals our most basic attitudes toward ourself, just as the kind of clothes we choose to wear reveals our attitudes toward our physical appearance. Much is made, in modern thought, of the impact of the clothes we wear. Certainly, if we wear rags and tattered garments, we put forth an image of poverty and a lack of self-respect. If we wear outrageous, tasteless, yet expensive clothes in an effort to attract attention to our status, we advertise our vanity and false pride. The well-dressed person avoids these extremes in favor of clothes which are stylish yet tasteful, discreet, and never extravagant. He takes pride in his appearance, but does not pretend to illusions of grandeur or jet-set elegance. He does not deceive himself, believing the clothes make the man, but he does know his outer garments are a useful means for expressing himself in daily life. They reveal his inner character.

Just so, our attitudes toward who we are and what we have done reveal the state of our psychological health and well-being. If we choose to belittle our accomplishments and deny our value as a human being, by dressing in false humility, we reveal for all to see the impoverishment of our life and our lack of concern for preserving our dignity. Even worse, if we wear the cloak of false humility as a badge of supposed spirituality, then we are playing the role of the "humble hypocrite," just as a rich man masquerading as a vagrant would be living a lie. On the other hand, if we exaggerate our achievements and try to impress people with our mental and physical superiority, we proclaim our conceit and arrogance. We may even be playing the dangerous game of setting the personality forth as more important than the soul, thereby alienating ourself from our inner greatness. We become a buffoon who cannot be taken seriously, because we are wearing the motley robes of a fool.

The truly humble person, by contrast, wears neither the sackcloth of worthlessness nor the robe of vanity. Instead, he wears a cloak befitting his dual role as a son of earth and a Son of heaven. He is aware of his talents, strengths, and responsibilities, and takes pride in them. But this pride never obscures his knowledge of the soul nor his service to its purpose. He walks with pride and humility both, in the light of his inner self.

Each of us has the right to wear this cloak. It is not for sale by any clothier, and cannot be seized or stolen. There is just one way of acquiring it, which is to adopt a proper attitude of humility and pride toward everything we do—treating others with respect, worshipping God as the one power of life, fulfilling our obligations at work with competence and dignity, contributing to the growth of civilization, and accepting the authority of the soul. For the cloak of humility is not just any garment, but a *robe without any seams, cut from cosmic fabric!* It is a perfect robe, and can only be acquired as we learn to honor and respect the potential for perfection within us. We are a divine creation, designed to become perfect even as our Father in heaven is perfect. We must therefore not deny our worth, or grovel in unwholesome contrition, or quail at the thought of our imperfections. There is no doubt that the personality makes mistakes from time to time; it is a necessary part of evolution. But even though the personality is not yet perfect, there is a part of us which is! There is a part of us, the soul, which is awesome in its talent, love, compassion, and wisdom. Our duty as a human being is to put on this robe without any seams and express our innate love, compassion, talent, and wisdom in every department of life. We are called to act with inspired humility.

The robe without any seams is a marvelous garment. It fills us with reverence for the presence of divine life wherever we may encounter it — in others, nature, the affairs of nations, the work of civilization, and all noble endeavors. It motivates us to engage our personality in the active expression of the very best elements within us. The more we wear it, and honor its purpose, the more we evolve into the kind of person who is *able* to contribute creatively to humanity and civilization, through our genius, love, and patient understanding.

This, then, is the most humble of all people: the person who unselfishly devotes himself to furthering the evolution of human life, because he loves God with all his heart and mind and soul and might, and has no thought but to serve Him fully and hallow His name with every breath of life.

By acting in these ways, we earn the right not only to wear the robe without any seams, but also to learn the proper posture of human enlightenment. And we prepare for the day when, proud and humble and deeply reverent, we meet God face to face.

A DIVISIVE FORCE

False humility in all its ugly distortions has been one of the favorite weapons of evil and malicious people in their struggle to manipulate and deceive the dedicated, spiritual people of the world, thereby gaining—or so they believe—an advantage. This is most clearly observed in religion, where the idea of humility has been seized by selfish, ill-hearted people seeking to insinuate themselves into positions of power in the organized church, so that they might pursue their mischief more easily. These people have twisted humility's original message of reverence and dignity into a poisonous concept of abasement, guilt, and inferiority. But the fair name and reputation of humility has been ravished in the field of politics as well, especially by those dark agents who have sought to conquer the masses by encouraging them to be jealous of those who have distinguished themselves.

Obviously, it is easier to control the masses of humanity if they have been schooled to be meek, submissive, untalented, unquestioning, and guilt-ridden. A flock of sheep is easily directed by the shepherd, whereas a group of intelligent individuals who are courageous enough to think and act for themselves is almost impossible to manipulate. Knowing this, selfish religious and political leaders have for eons used false versions of humility to enslave and exploit their followers. As a result, the pace of human evolution has been slowed, freedoms denied, and much human suffering inflicted.

The means used by these exploiters to cripple our courage and dignity are many and varied. One of the most devious has been the misrepresentation of humility as meekness. For generations, we have been taught that humility is a lowly state—a state in which we are painfully aware of our manifold flaws and lack of power. Unworthy and insignificant, we are reduced to begging God to give us a scrap of dignity. Then, once our pitiful plea is spoken, the religious or political leaders step in and inform us that *their* power is the dignity we have been praying for. In this way, our personal strength is destroyed and meekness is perpetuated. Humility has been cleverly used to humiliate us and make it almost impossible to approach God successfully. The terrible consequences of this tragedy can perhaps be most clearly understood if we remember that God approaches us on wavelengths of benevolence, wisdom, and courage. As long as we are stuck on small thoughts of lowliness, fear, and weakness, *we deny ourself the companionship of God!*

This approach has been so effective in enslaving the minds of mankind that even today the majority of us spend much of our time trying to "out-meek" one another. But because such behavior runs counter to the design and purpose of mankind, it is always a pretense and illusion. We succeed only in becoming "humble hypocrites" who are vulnerable to any power-hungry individual who wishes to dominate us.

A byproduct of this perversion of humility is the pagan worship of guilt and sin so commonly found in Western religions. By constantly emphasizing the grossness of our errors and sins, the vandals of the spiritual life have cheapened our sense of self-worth—all in the holy name of humility. Worship has become, for many, nothing more than an act of groveling in contrition and the confession of sins and inadequacies. Instead of approaching God with love and filling our heart with beauty, we are encouraged to retreat from His presence in fear and trembling. Almost by sleight of hand, we are kept from discovering God's true nature—the nature of His love, wisdom, and power.

Indeed, in the hands of malicious people, false humility becomes a powerfully divisive force, a wedge driven between us and the very presence of life. It is also frequently used to divide us one from another. After all, if we are taught to feel guilty because another human being has not been as successful as we have been, it is only natural to start resenting and despising this other person—not because of his weaknesses, but because of our guilt. Once again, false humility has been subtly used to manipulate us and harm the quality of our life.

Yet another mischievous misuse of the ideal of humility is the quasi-religious notion that a strong sense of individuality will impair our capacity to reunite with God. The advocates of this philosophy encourage us to "get the self out of the way" so divine influences can flow through us without "interference." It sounds like a good idea, yet the consequences of following this admonition are disastrous! If we actually did succeed in getting the self out of the way, it would be the equivalent of committing psychological suicide—a total denial of our individuality, talents, destiny, and duties. It would reduce our personal importance to the lowest possible level, transforming us into a passive dummy. Some people do believe this is what God wants us to be. But if God had wanted the earth to be a colony of passive dummies, He certainly would have been clever enough to create a race of automatons—not human beings with a free will and a mind.

It is the devotees of psychological suicide who have created the notion that pride is a sin. To them, polite behavior and contrite worship of God are infinitely preferable to inspired contributions to civilization or dedicated good works. In the end, they are intimidated by competence, beauty, wisdom—and God Himself. And so they try to tear down the good works of others in a fit of inferiority and martyrdom. Ironically, they become totally unfit to serve as channels of divine inspiration. Since they have little individuality left, they lack the means with which to shape a meaningful expression of any divine attribute.

But perhaps the most destructive disfigurement of humility occurs when incompetent people and petty organizations use it to sabotage the efforts of other, more skillful people. Jealous of the authority, intelligence, or creative talent of anyone else, these people attack competent individuals with charges of arrogance and pride—simply as a means of sidetracking them from their work! Inwardly they hope their own lack of talent or power will be less obvious as a result.

This problem is more pervasive than many goodhearted people are willing to admit, because they, too, have been conditioned by the untalented people of the world to believe in this type of humility—this wretched humility which equates competence with arrogance, success with pride, wealth with evil, and power with abuse. But let no one be deceived—every creative, inspired, and enlightened person who has ever walked openly among the masses of mankind has tasted of this opposition and knows how bitter it is. The reputations of many of civilization's greatest supporters and geniuses have been damaged past repair for no other reason than the jealousy and pettiness of incompetent people who chose to attack them rather than do something worthwhile of their own. As the English poet Dame Edith Sitwell has put it: "It is imagined, for some reason, that it is perfectly right and proper for persons of small wit, and a dreadful little slick talent, or indeed, for persons of no wit, and not even that pimpish talent, to attack, and try to injure, any creature possessed of genius. It does not matter how low and foul the attack, it does not matter by what cunning, hatred, and malice it may be prompted, nor how under-brained and dirty the attacker may be. The quarry is possessed of genius, and is therefore meant to be hunted and half-killed. But let a man of genius reply, and the whole populace rises up to protect the original aggressor."

"Humility" is a word which is easily invoked by people who feel inferior and want to justify their inadequacies. By making a virtue of the lack of success and disguising it as humility, they gain recognition without achievement—and the praise of others who likewise delight in obvious rationalizations. Unfortunately, when society endorses this childish behavior it simultaneously endorses the perpetuation of pettiness and mediocrity. When society's geniuses are humiliated and the unproductive masses are subsidized and indulged as a regular practice, how can civilization avoid sinking into a quicksand pit of triviality and incompetence? The situation is not so much pathetic as it is bathetic. The quality of everyone's life deteriorates and suffers.

Lest we forget, it was precisely this distortion of humility which led to the crucifixion of the Christ. He was betrayed not just by Judas but even more so by the weakness of the crowds of Jerusalem, who were manipulated by the Pharisees and Sadducees into believing the Christ to be arrogant and proud—to have claimed He was King of the Jews. Jesus claimed no such thing, *but the mere power of His presence, His ability to heal, and His obvious wisdom were sufficiently superior that the crowd was willing to believe Him to be arrogant.* In modern times, it is this sense of inferiority which motivates many Marxists, cultists, and other paranoids to attack the worthwhile foundations of society in general and the outstanding achievements of creative geniuses in particular.

The effort to destroy competence, to make us feel inadequate, to burden us with unworthiness and guilt, and to enshrine meekness is an evil one and should be recognized as such. It is important for intelligent people of goodwill throughout the world to join together in combating these distortions of humility and pride. To paraphrase Edmund Burke, the only thing necessary for the triumph of evil is for good people to believe they are unworthy of God's love and grace. Nothing entraps us more than falling victim to *any* form of false humility. A sense of worthlessness impoverishes our consciousness. The conviction of incompetence stifles growth and self-improvement. Self-effacement exposes us to manipulation, exploitation, and even attack by selfish, petty people. Self-denial betrays the divine elements within us as much as it suppresses the imperfect ones. But worst of all, the cloak of false humility drains the vitality of the life force from us. We progressively become more dull and lifeless, until we not only are living a petty life, but an insipid one as well. Like vampires who suck the blood of their victims, the apostles of meekness, the princes of pettiness, and the protectors of incompetence suck the lifeblood of our creative genius, spiritual endowment, and will to achieve. If, then, we willingly surrender to this dissipation of our livingness, we condemn ourself to being little more than a puppet of unholy forces. If we abandon God, what will fill the void?

There is only one way to stop those who profit from the distortion of humility, and that is to honor and support its proper and enlightened uses. We must not be fooled by their half-truths and slimy misrepresentations. When they tell us to fear God, we must remember that genuine humility enhances the quality of life and makes us more responsive to our inner spiritual heritage. When they lecture us about pride, we must recall that humility supports achievement and growth and teaches us the value of becoming a more competent journeyman in the art of living. When they condemn the geniuses and wise thinkers of the world, we must keep in mind that true humility does not belittle or degrade; it helps us respect genius and creativity, our own and that of others. When they tell us to get the self out of the way, we must stand up to the full height of our humanity and tell them: "We *are* the way the light of the soul shines into the world!"

We must take pride in the expression of inspired humility.

OUR RIGHTFUL PLACE

The heart of humility is the establishment of a proper relationship between the personality and the soul. The person who refuses to admit the reality of the soul is very unhumble and arrogant, and severely limited in his capacity to grow. The person who distorts the nature of the soul by fearing it and groveling before it is likewise quite unhumble. But the individual who knows the soul to be a divine portion of God intent upon working in the manifest worlds, and the personality to be the beloved creation of the soul, has learned the most important lesson of humility. He is able to acknowledge the authority, love, and wisdom of the soul while also appreciating the noble role the personality is designed to perform. With this understanding, he is ready to begin transforming his attitudes, beliefs, and habits so they become a direct expression of the wisdom, love, and nobility of the soul.

None of this involves abasing the personality in any way. In fact, the effect on the personality is the exact opposite; as a true relationship is established with the soul, through the practice of inspired humility, the role of the personality is expanded. It is enriched. We become more sure of our skills, strengths, worth, and intelligence. We become more acquainted with the love and benevolence of the inner being. And we find that the clarification of this one, great relationship leads to a better understanding of many other important relationships, too.

We discover, for example, that we can have a meaningful relationship with the universe. The soul lives and moves and has its being within a much greater Life, the universe. Through our relationship with the soul, established by the practice of inspired humility, we are able to make contact with the divine forces which comprise the universe—the forces of pure wisdom, goodwill, joy, order, peace, and will. These forces are the divine archetypes of life, imperishable and perfect. They are the source of the highest level of human inspiration. If we believe ourself unworthy of contacting them, we will be unable to relate to them. If we arrogantly dismiss them as unreal and unimportant, we will severely restrict our capacity to comprehend life. But if we approach them with true humility, we will gain access to a universe of inspiration and power.

We will also find that inspired humility helps us relate more constructively with other people, both at the inner and the outer levels. Our relationship with our own soul will enable us to build useful relationships with the inner beings of our friends, relatives, colleagues, and acquaintances. As we explore these transcendent relationships, our capacity to treat our friends and colleagues with affection, understanding, and joy will increase tremendously. We will discover new meaning in the idea of *respecting* others. This, in turn, will enrich the quality of our relationship with their outer dimensions. At these levels, however, the way we deal with others will vary greatly, from one person to the next, depending on the nature of their character. The true nature of humility demands it.

If, for example, a friend behaves childishly, we would treat him as we would treat a child. To pretend he was behaving like an adult would be false humility. Of course, the friend might construe this response to be arrogant, but then childish minds usually have difficulty comprehending humility.

Similarly, if an individual behaves stupidly or incompetently, it would betray the spirit of humility to pretend that he is a wise or skilled person. By the same token, it would be cruel to humiliate or embarrass him in any way. Instead, we should reject both these extremes and treat the fellow with kindness, encouraging him to see the sad results of his incompetence and work to improve himself and his skills. At times it may be necessary to handle an incompetent person firmly—perhaps even rebuking him—but if we are genuinely humble, we will always act compassionately to help him expand his abilities. We will refrain from treating him condescendingly.

By contrast, when we encounter people with obviously greater wisdom, love, or skill, the spirit of humility should move us to recognize their superiority and cherish it. There is no need to grovel before it or feel inferior by comparison—this would be false humility. Nor should we worship them as though they were gods or heroes—this would be unseemly. Instead, we should delight in their accomplishments and be inspired by their genius. We should make it a point of honor to assist them in whatever ways we can, and defend them against the attacks of unhumble people who falsely malign them with charges of arrogance and pride, simply because they do their work well and with inspiration.

Another important relationship which is clarified by the humble approach to life is our attitude toward the impulse to serve humanity and civilization. There are many people "on the spiritual path" who are quite willing to believe that everything they do serves God. In most cases, however, it is only their vanities they serve. They act for fame, self-aggrandizement, and the control of the minds of impressionable people—not for the glory of God. Others turn their back on the value of service, and absorb themselves in the pursuit of selfishness. But these attitudes estrange us from our human dignity. If we are humble, we stand ready to dedicate our energies to serving God and man, because we know that service enriches the abundance of life for all. It is an active expression of respect and reverence for God's Plan.

The practice of inspired humility also gives us the capacity to sense the proper relationship between the daily events of our life and national, planetary, and even cosmic events. Out of context, our solitary life has no meaning or value. It is our interaction with our nation, with human civilization, and with the life of God which gives purpose and relevance to our individuality—and makes our personal freedom and self-expression worth cherishing. Knowing this, the humble person does not clamor for "personal rights" at the expense of universal good—but neither does he succumb to the illusion of believing that his life is pointless. He rejects both of these extremes as vanities, and embraces the role of enlightened citizenship with humility.

In each of these kinds of relationship, the power of humility is that it helps us establish our rightful place— with the soul, in the universe, with others, as an agent of God, and as a citizen of life. It gives us definition and a sense of posture, enabling us to stand and honor our obligations. A humble attitude serves the important function of reminding us, always, of the centrality of divine life, and helps us recognize the influence of divine forces in our life, the world, and the universe. Our thinking is not clouded with the selfish, arrogant concerns of protecting our prejudices or defending our vanities. Instead of being preoccupied with petty issues and irrelevant obsessions, we are able to rise above them and appreciate our opportunities for sharing in divine purposes, plans, and principles. Humility magnifies our perception of priorities, preparing us to act more wisely.

It must be borne in mind, however, that inspired humility is much more than just an attitude: it is a motivation for acting in daily life as well. Inspired by humility, we are able to discern the true value of the divine qualities of life and our proper relationship with them—but until we act *to honor* these qualities in our daily life, the promise of humility is only partly fulfilled.

Having discovered for ourself the ideal of beauty, for example, humility then leads us to honor beauty by supporting the arts, admiring the genius of people who have revealed beauty in their own life, and cultivating a sense of beauty of our own.

Having been inspired in our thoughts by the evolutionary nature of human life, humility leads us to honor this fundamental impulse by promoting competence in education, encouraging true scientific investigation, and pursuing enlightenment ourself.

Having discovered for ourself the presence of divine life throughout the universe, humility leads us to honor this presence of divinity by finding it and loving it in every divine creature — our friends, our colleagues, everyone we deal with, animals, plants, and Mother Nature herself. We treat other people with integrity and goodwill. We treat nature with a sense of stewardship and responsibility. We refrain from manipulating, cheating, embarrassing, or exploiting others, and stand firm when others try to act in those ways. When honor requires it, we are unafraid to expose the weaknesses of others, but in every circumstance, we are guided by the inner life of the people we deal with — indeed, the inner life of the planet itself.

There always remains the temptation, of course, to honor a false ideal. In addition, the decisions we will have to make at times will be most bewildering. A business person may be tempted, for example, to put profits ahead of divine ideals. A labor union might encourage its members to place self-serving concerns above the economic and political welfare of their country. A minister or priest might become more concerned with collecting the offering than with offering charity and guidance. But the principles of humility and honor will guide us to the right decisions, if we turn to them. If we humble ourself before the ideals of the inner being and the purposes of God, we will have little trouble making intelligent choices in most cases.

The principle of acting with honor applies to groups and nations as well as individuals. Not enough is said and written in these modern times about the need for collective honor; we become absorbed too easily in organizational braggadocio and unjustified national pride. Not even religions are exempt from these vanities, with most sects claiming to have sole possession of the one right path to salvation, heaven, enlightenment, or whatever the final goal of perfection is called. If these groups would stop bickering and condemning and begin *honoring* the ideals of spiritual aspiration, they would discover that the principle they are meant to serve is *loving service*. Only when a religious group embraces this ideal does it become truly humble.

Among political groups, the ideal is *citizenship*. The honorable political party, therefore, is the one which serves the best interests of its nation above all other concerns. At the national level, the ideal is the *evolution* of civilization, through international cooperation. If countries spent less time bragging about their superiority and howling about their petty interests, they would have more time to concentrate on advancing the causes of civilization. This act of inspired humility would magnify their standing among the community of nations.

Even on cosmic levels, it is universal honor which promotes inspired humility. It stretches the human mind to think in terms of cosmic humility and honor, but the very existence of life in any corner of the universe, including earth, depends on it. God, too, honors and loves His purpose and value, thereby nurturing life.

Let us therefore do as God does, and honor and love our divine worth. There are imperfections in our life, just as there are imperfections in the larger dimensions of life. But we are meant to correct them, patiently, and create perfection in their stead. We cannot begin, however, until we recognize that we are involved in God's life.

The proper work of mankind involves us in a noble mission to glorify heaven on earth. Each of us has a significant role to play in this work. Guided by inspired humility—a sense of worth and personal honor— we can individually justify God's involvement with us.

LOVING GOD

Inspired humility focuses on the positive elements of life, encouraging us to think well of ourself, others, God, and civilization. Since most of us *want* to think well of ourself and life, it is not hard to learn the lessons of inspired humility—once we understand what it is. The greater difficulty is *unlearning* what we have been taught about false humility and repairing the damage incurred in our self-image, attitudes, and pride. To succeed, we will have to develop a capacity to discriminate between the elements of life which are worthy of respect and reverence, and those which are not. We will have to learn the distinction between pride and vanity, humility and self-denial, and conceit and a healthy self-regard. We are called to *glorify* the personality as a noble creation of the soul—but must take care not to *glamorize* it. It is one thing to recognize and express the worth of our ideas and accomplishments, but quite another to imagine ourself a newly-born Apollo or Venus.

In short, it is desirable to know we have important work to do, recognize what it is, and set to the task of completing it. It is not desirable, however, to take out full-page advertisements in the local newspaper announcing how wonderful we are and how everyone should appreciate the work we are doing.

Above all, we must be honest with ourself. We cannot become humble without contemplating our true nature and worth, as a means of discerning the importance of what we do and what we can achieve. But if we let a lust for fame or approval intrude into our contemplations, we are apt to deceive ourself, believing our importance to be a good deal greater than it actually is. Such a belief, of course, is an act of vanity. Instead of wanting to stand upright as an honorable human being, we are more interested in strutting like a child who has just become king of the mountain.

In understanding our true worth, it is best to keep focused on the divine elements within us, as this will help us avoid the pitfall of conceit. If we dwell on the superficial aspects of our individuality—physical beauty, athletic accomplishments, business successes, mental prowess—we will most likely end up indulging in self-congratulation. In any event, we will not discover our true nature and worth, which far transcend these transient appearances. Therefore, we should seek out first the higher worth of our soul, realizing that we are a divine creature, a child of God who arrived on earth *with the seeds of greatness already within us!* These seeds exist in our inmost self; as the personality increases its capacity to recognize them, we find the key to our highest potential and value. With this realization, we are then able to unlock the power and wisdom of the soul and use them to inspire our mind, abilities, and love.

The immanence of these divine seeds guarantees that our basic nature is essentially good, no matter how much we may have rejected or obscured this goodness in daily life. To be sure, some people do believe men and women to be inherently evil, at least in part, but this is a very arrogant idea. It is a vanity and an illusion—and a most destructive one. There is, of course, a part of us which is often stupid, mischievous, and incompetent—but this is only the portion of our personality not yet dominated by our soul. The soul itself is always pure—and worthy of our humble reverence. If we believe we are inherently evil, we cannot properly honor the *greatness* within us; if we believe we are by nature worthless or insignificant, we cannot glorify the *divine* seeds within us.

Once we perceive our divine nature and worth, the next step in developing inspired humility is honoring this inner greatness in all we do. Our goal in this step is to plant the seeds of love and wisdom in the fertile earth of our daily life. We must also train ourself never to deny our worth through our actions, thoughts, or wishes.

Because our life has a noble purpose, for example, we should recognize that the work we do to earn our daily bread is noble, too. Many people deprecate the value of their work, grumbling and complaining about it, but this cynical attitude diminishes their human worth as well. The humble attitude is to recognize that the service we perform or the product we manufacture is of value to others and to civilization. Our own role in producing the final goods or service may be large or small, but is nonetheless a necessary contribution. And we should be justly proud of it.

For the same reason, our human relationships are of great value. Our friends and loved ones probably are not world famous, or movers of society, but still they possess the same divine elements in their soul that we and everyone else do. And so, we should cherish them for what they are and what they can become. We know they have imperfections and irritating habits, but by acting with inspired humility, we can easily see the emerging goodness within them. If we honor this, the value of our relationships will appreciate many times over in a relatively short time.

There are simple ways to honor our inner worth, too. When someone pays us a well-deserved compliment, we should not be embarrassed by it and say, "Oh, it was nothing." It was *not* nothing—it was an expression of our human worth! To pretend it was nothing is to sink into false humility. A truly humble response is to say: "Thank you, I'm glad you appreciate it." And then we should silently thank our inner being for assisting and guiding us in this success.

Due to the pervasiveness of false humility, we daily deny our inner worth in too many ways to catalogue here. When we do, we are in essence denying the Christ within us—the presence of consciousness within us which is trying to magnify and enrich the quality of our life. Whenever we refuse a reasonable challenge to grow in competence or educate ourself, preferring the comfort of the status quo, we are denying the Christ. Whenever we pretend we cannot act in loving ways or achieve a greater spiritual expression, we are denying the Christ. Whenever we treat other people in dishonorable ways, thus denying their worth and value, we deny the Christ. Whenever we deride the accomplishments of geniuses and the legitimate advances of civilization, we again deny the Christ. And, we are denying our own capacity to grow. We are failing in our efforts to develop inspired humility.

Therefore, we must also adopt the habit of aspiring for the very highest and best. A central part of humility is recognizing that *we deserve the best* — not necessarily in physical goods, but most assuredly the best opportunities to express our talents, the best qualities of character, the best health, and the best relationships. We must not, however, succumb to the vanity of believing these favorable conditions will come to us automatically. We deserve the best of everything in life *because we have the inner capacity to attract the best, stir up the most noble, and express the greatest talents and qualities — if we work at it.* As long as we brood on our faults and failures, our consciousness sinks in quality. But when we aspire to the best, in order to honor the divine elements within us more fully, we learn the secret of cooperating with life.

As might be expected, it is likewise important to aspire for the best in others, our work, society, and civilization. Instead of looking for elements to criticize, deprecating the efforts of others, pessimistically clucking about the doom of civilization, and hoping God will smite our enemies or destroy the world, the humble approach to life is to nurture goodness wherever we find it, trust in the competence of others and society, and cooperate with the highest ideals of civilization. Naturally, there will be times when mistakes are made by others, when our trust is compromised, and when cooperation brings betrayal. The humble person does not pretend such things never happen, because they do. Yet he realizes it is his job to confront imperfection and correct it — not by emphasizing the problem but by honoring the perfection which can eventually be attained. Complaining about imperfection does not fulfill our basic mission as a human being; neither does running away from it. Our task is consummated only by rendering the imperfect more perfect.

In developing humility, we must also take care not to equate the posture of humility with submissiveness. Submissiveness and self-effacement are variations of false humility. As such, they should be avoided by every intelligent person. Because there are many people in the world who still practice false humility, however, we must be aware that there will be times when others *expect us* to be submissive and meek—so they can manipulate us. When we then respond with an appropriate measure of self-worth and refuse to be intimidated, they will accuse us of lacking humility, being arrogant, and affecting superiority. Without becoming paranoid, we must nonetheless be strong enough in character to stand up to these people and not let them humiliate the divine elements within us. We must be prepared not to deny carelessly the Christ within us, by caving in to such accusations in the name of "politeness." There is nothing spiritual about surrendering our dignity just to make some snivelling worm feel good. Indeed, it destroys the fabric of our integrity and leads to a progressive loss of standing in the community of mankind.

Just so, an integral part of attaining humility is defending those who revere life from the attacks of vain and malicious people. Those individuals who make the greatest contributions to human civilization and thought often experience great opposition, criticism, or frustration in bringing their works to the unhumble masses. We may not be prepared at this time to make a contribution equal to theirs, but we always have the opportunity—nay, the duty—to champion their work, celebrate their accomplishments, take pride in their humanity, and defend them against attack and deprecation.

Ultimately, all suggestions for developing inspired

humility reduce to one factor: we must learn to love God more completely. This does not necessarily mean going to church more often or praying more frequently. Our best opportunity for loving God is always in the moment-to-moment activity of our life. We love God by respecting and honoring whatsoever is good, noble, and perfect. We love God by recognizing His presence wherever we go and by abiding in that presence reverently.

Unfortunately, many people manage to distort even such a simple idea as loving God. Instead of revering the goodly qualities and sublime beauties of life, they dedicate themselves to fearing what is evil. Yet fearing evil is not the opposite side of the coin of loving good. The opposite of loving good is hating good; fearing evil, by contrast, is the opposite of *loving evil.* And whether a person spends his time loving or fearing evil makes little difference—he is still directing his attention toward evil. He is filling his mind with thoughts of evil and polluting his aura with images of it, and as a result, his consciousness sinks in quality, no matter how good his intentions may be. Indeed, some of the religious people who quite sincerely spend their time fearing evil eventually become magnetically entranced by it, thereby losing their sense of discrimination.

It must be clearly understood that as long as our imagination and fears are filled with the shadow of evil, we cannot walk in the presence of God. We must maintain a healthy awareness that there are evil currents in the world which must be opposed, to be sure, but our mind, heart, and soul should be affixed to the contemplation of the divine, the wonderful, and the inspiring!

This is the proper occupation for the humble person.

KNOWING GOD

As these simple steps for increasing humility are practiced, many changes in our outlook, character, and behavior gradually occur. We learn to stand erect—the natural posture for the enlightened human being. Centered in dignity and nobility, we become a strong person. We give over our meek and groveling ways. No more do we have to be constantly crushed in contrition, reduced to begging for forgiveness. We are strong enough to be forgiving and kind, helping those who are still weak in spirit to learn to stand. We are strong enough to be cooperative, conciliatory, and helpful. Instead of asserting rage, anger, or paranoia— which any weak or bewildered person can express— we are strong enough to assert our goodwill and humanity.

Inspired by humility, we are strong enough to dedicate our life to acting rightly, to behaving responsibly, to treating other people fairly, and to standing firmly in the face of opposition. When our personal strength falters, humility helps us remember we are never alone; we derive our true strength from the wisdom, love, and order of our inner being. So we turn to this inner companion and honor it anew, by focusing its light into the difficult areas of our life. We look for the good elements of life and expect them, even as we expect to be productive, useful, and helpful in life. This is the attitude which gives birth to good opportunities.

Endowed with humility, we are strong enough to respond to the failures of life with wisdom and integrity. Instead of sinking into a state of despair and anger, we admit the failure and try to learn something of value from it—some positive quality which will help us become more competent, more understanding, more discerning, or more loving, so we will not fail again in the future. Similarly, we are strong enough to respond to criticism with thoughtful evaluation. Where we can learn from criticism, we make appropriate adjustments in attitude, thought, or behavior. But we do not let critical words tear apart our self-esteem; being humble, we honor our own values, sense of worth, and ideals.

Knowing that honest self-expression is something to be proud of, we act in life by investing our humanity — not by rejecting opportunities. We do not timidly stand back in the shadows; we are strong enough to plunge forth into the adventure of life and partake of our portion of it. And we are likewise strong enough that we do not have to try to escape the hardships of life or anesthetize our feelings of unworthiness; whether at work or play, we are able to celebrate life.

Having learned that the inner life of God always seeks to glorify us rather than make us slaves of fear, we look for and find the presence of God — whether we label it this or not — in all we do, in everyone we deal with, and in every opportunity which comes to us. We respect it, protect it, and encourage its successful expression in daily life.

There have been many people throughout the history of mankind who have lived this portrait of inspired humility. In some cases their names are remembered; in some they are not. One of the most sublime examples was a Carmelite monk named Brother Lawrence who lived in the seventeenth century in France and left behind a small body of writings called *The Practice of the Presence of God*. Brother Lawrence rejected the conventional religious expressions of "humility" of his day, such as mortification of the body and self-denial, and advanced the philosophy that the sign of true humility was a constant interest in communing with divine life, not just in quiet moments of prayer, but even more importantly during moments of "outward employment" and active living. Any human being has the capacity to live in this presence of God, he professed, because "our sanctification does not depend upon *changing* our works, but in doing for God's sake that which we commonly do for our own." He understood as well that loving God is the principal means of coming within the grace of His aura. "We must *know* before we can *love*. In order to *know* God, we must often *think* of Him; and when we come to *love* Him, we shall then also *think* of Him often, for our heart will be with our treasure."

Only when we have magnified our humanity to its greatest degree, through inspired humility, can we know God.

HUMBLING OURSELF

Because inspired humility magnifies the good qualities of life, it can be applied to the art of living in very sensible and practical ways. Humility helps us discover the transcendent elements in life, honor them, and help them grow. It gives us a way to lift the fabric of our life out of the realm of pettiness into a genuine significance.

As we humble ourself before the transcendent elements in our marriage bond, for example, we find it much easier to be tolerant of the imperfections in the relationship. Seeing them more clearly, it is then easier and less threatening to work at diminishing them — and at reducing the stress and tension accompanying them. The transcendent qualities of a marriage would include love, loyalty, companionship, harmony, affection, cooperation, and much more.

We should also humble ourself before the transcendent purpose of our work. For social workers, teachers, and many others, this transcendent purpose is serving humanity. For doctors and other health professionals, it is healing humanity by nurturing the spirit's ideal for form and function. For lawyers, it is justice. For scientists, it is the discovery and comprehension of the phenomena of nature. For statesmen, it is inspired leadership. For performers, it is grace and beauty. For businessmen, it is the responsible management of human and natural resources. For skilled workers, it is competent productivity. For farmers, it is the principle of sustaining life. By honoring this purpose in the way we conduct our work, we lift our efforts out of the ordinary and instill them with something extra. We discover creative new ways to fulfill our duties—and find much more satisfaction in them. After all, this is why genuine humility is called *inspired* humility—because it brings with it fresh inspiration which lets us act creatively.

We should humble ourself before the transcendent impulse of causes we are devoted to. If involved in volunteer work, for example, it will be much more satisfying to identify with the purpose being served by this work—and not with the status it brings us, or the influential people we meet, or the parties that are thrown to raise money. Devotion to favored causes often generates excessive fanaticism (as can be seen in religion and politics), but the truly humble person will not be prejudiced by this fanaticism, because he understands the underlying value of the cause—and respects it enough not to pollute it with frenzy or foolishness.

We should humble ourself before the spirit of our community and nation, trying to understand the contributions it seeks to make. In America, for example, one of the purposes of the national spirit is to inspire the citizens of the country to demonstrate the nature of enlightened citizenship for all the world to witness. Arrogant citizens who are too proud to participate in the life of their country—or too conceited to participate *intelligently*—interfere with the fulfillment of this transcendent purpose. But those who love their national community respect its purposes and help promote them. In this manner, humility enriches their lives.

We should humble ourself before the transcendent brilliance of inspired art, music, literature, and drama. Part of this application of humility is rejecting insipid, stupid, and childish forms of art, music, and literature that do not embody the divine elements of beauty.

We should humble ourself before the glories of nature. It is said that Brother Lawrence devoted his life to the love of God because he was moved by the sight of a barren tree in winter and the subsequent realization that it would shortly be renewed to life by the touch of the divine presence of God.

We should humble ourself before outstanding examples of human talent and achievement—in athletics, business, science, the arts, self-awareness, motherhood, and the performance of duty. We should avoid jealousy and envy, which humiliate our own worth.

We should humble ourself before the benevolence of the universe, which affords us so many opportunities for growth. We should become aware of the inner forces urging us, even forcing us, to grow and increase our competence. Instead of fighting them, which only leads to stress, we should honor these impulses of destined perfection.

We should humble ourself before the transcendent qualities of friendship, because friendship is one of the most meaningful and durable ways to express the presence of God in our own life. The qualities of friendship include loyalty, cooperation, harmony, and empathy.

We should humble ourself before our ideal self-image, which is cut from cosmic fabric.

We should humble ourself before perfection, knowing there does not exist an area of life which cannot be made perfect.

But we should never humble ourself before the imperfect, the cunning, the manipulative, the intimidating, the incompetent, the low in spirit, the chaotic, or anything evil. In the presence of these elements, we must assert our strength and humble ourself only to the omnipresence of God.

Applying inspired humility to even the tiniest element of our life creates in our personality a channel through which we can direct inspiration. Thus, we enlighten the earth and anoint our own individuality. We consecrate the personality.

As a human being, we are designed to be happy, to be pleased with the significant role we play in the universe, and to be fruitful. As we discover the seeds of consciousness which are to be developed in our earthly life, we are meant to plant them, care for them, and multiply them. Through humility, we are given a means to magnify these elements of consciousness and use them to create a proper life expression.

Inspired humility, therefore, is a means of liberating the spirit which has been entrapped by meekness, vanities, urges which pull us downward, and contrition. Freed from these limitations, our dignity, joy, and intelligence can more fully express our greatness.

What is true of the individual is likewise true of groups and nations. Countries are seldom enslaved by other nations—they are enslaved instead by their own attitudes, selfishness, meekness, and contrition. When the national character has been poisoned from within, it is easier for outside forces to manipulate, intimidate, and dominate. But when a nation has become strong through humility—by humbling itself to the purpose of its spirit, the worth of civilization, the goodness in other nations, and the presence of God, then it is truly blessed with inalienable freedoms.

At its most sublime level, humility helps us step out of the personal shell of our little existence and become universal, even cosmic, in our participation in life. It becomes a continuous act of celebrating the presence of God, and unites us with the highest elements of God's life. Such union is only possible, however, if we realize that we are well-loved sons and daughters of God, and all which is His is ours as well. If we are too meek to claim these treasures, or too weak to defend them from outrage and abuse, then we do not know God very well, and cannot hope to love Him. But if we truly humble ourself before the greatness within us, and love life well enough to express this greatness through our activities, then we inherit His treasures.

In this thought lies the true interpretation of the fifth Beatitude, which is sometimes translated: "Blessed are the meek, for they shall inherit the earth." What a terrible distortion this choice of words gives to the intention of the Christ! Meekness does not bless—it curses life. A far more accurate translation is: "Blessed are they who bring the life of spirit to earth, for they shall inherit its treasures."

The legacy of humility is rich indeed.

ABOUT THE AUTHORS

In the late 1960's, Dr. Robert R. Leichtman's interest in intuition and spiritual growth caused him to close his medical practice and devote his energies to personal psychic work, lecturing, teaching, and writing. His pioneer work as a psychic consultant to psychiatrists, psychologists, and medical doctors has helped him become recognized as one of the premier psychics in America today. He is also the developer of "Active Meditation," a comprehensive course in personal growth and meditative techniques. Dr. Leichtman currently resides in Baltimore, where part of his time is spent participating, with Olga Worrall, in the healing services of the New Life Clinic.

A graduate of Dartmouth College, Carl Japikse began his work career as a newspaper reporter and freelance writer. He has worked for several newspapers, including *The Wall Street Journal*. In the early 1970's, he left the field of journalism to pursue his current interests: teaching "Active Meditation" and other courses in personal growth, writing, lecturing, and consulting psychically with businesses and individuals. Mr. Japikse is the developer of "The Enlightened Management Seminar," an educational program for executives and managers, and various courses in spiritual growth.

Dr. Leichtman and Mr. Japikse are also the authors of *The Life of Spirit,* an essay series on spiritual themes, and *Forces of the Zodiac,* a monthly psychological forecast. Both of these series are published by Ariel Press and issued by subscription. Dr. Leichtman is the author of yet another series published by Ariel Press, *From Heaven to Earth,* a series of 24 interviews with the spirits of famous individuals.

THE WORK OF LIGHT

The Art of Living is issued by Ariel Press, the publishing house of Light, a nonprofit, charitable foundation.

The purpose of Light is to stimulate the growth of the mind and the creativity of people throughout the world. It was founded by Dr. Robert R. Leichtman and Carl Japikse, two authorities on human consciousness, personal growth, and the creative process. The work of Light is to enrich the human capacity to use the mind and spirit wisely and productively.

The activities of Light include the publications of Ariel Press, a series of taped lectures, the development of new classes, the Books of Light book club, and the presentation of lectures and forums.

Contributing members of the work of Light receive a series of lessons in personal growth called *Enlightenment*. Each issue of *Enlightenment* focuses on one specific aspect of the development of the mind. creativity, or the intuition. In addition, members receive a newsletter, "The Work of Light," and automatically become members of Books of Light.

The cost of a contributing membership is $25 a year for an individual, $40 a year for a family. There are also three other levels of contributing membership: the *fellow*, who contributes $100 a year; the *benefactor*, who contributes $250 a year; and the *angel*, who contributes $1,000 a year. Fellows, benefactors, and angels receive all membership benefits, plus a 20 percent discount on books purchased from Ariel Press during the year.

To become a contributing member of Light, send a check to Light, 2557 Wickliffe Road, Columbus, Ohio 43221-1899. Contributions to the work of Light are fully tax-deductible.

THE ART OF LIVING

Volume I, containing the first six essays in this series, and Volume II, containing essays seven through twelve, are both available in paperback editions similar to this one, from the publisher for $5.95 plus $1 for postage and handling. Other essays are still available in pamphlet form and can be ordered individually for $1.95 apiece, plus 55¢ for postage.

The whole series, including Volume III (this book) is available for $35, postpaid. To order the whole series *except* Volume III, the price is $28, postpaid. If ordering the whole series minus Volume III, please specify that you do not want Volume III.

Orders can be placed by sending a check for the appropriate amount with typed or printed instructions to Ariel Press, 2557 Wickliffe Road, Columbus, Ohio 43221-1899. Ohio residents please add 5½% sales tax. For foreign delivery, please add $3 to your order.